Jus

Please return/renew this item by the last date shown.
Items may also be renewed by the internet*

https://library.eastriding.gov.uk

* Please note a PIN will be required to access this service
- this can be obtained from your library

ISBN: 978-0-244-01836-8

PublishNation
www.publishnation.co.uk

Acknowledgements: *(in no particular order)*
All those who took the trouble to come out and visit me on the trip: Tasha, my folks and step folks (and Tiny), Mickey B & Hayley, Sophy & Dan (& Ezra) Lou, Paddy. Friends and family who stayed in contact throughout including Bruv & Tom and my lovely grandparents. All the people I met along the way that helped make this trip so wonderful.

Special Thanks: *To Teddy, Malcy and Hayley, for helping to proof reid this docament. Fore you're through apraoch in leafing no stone inturned. I feil so confadint that its all prefect with no misteaks - Fanks so much, your brillent prove reiders. I owe you a bear.*

Disclaimer: This book was written using notes made during the walk and from memory. It's therefore possible that I've got a few things muddled, chronologically speaking. A certain cove or cliff appearing in the wrong order, that sort of thing. As you will realise soon enough, I also have no idea what I'm talking about regards species identification, both animal and plant, so I've probably got some of that wrong as well. In summary, if you read the book accepting that your narrator is an idiot that doesn't know what he's talking about, you'll be fine.

Contents

Prologue

Daylight at last begins to creep under the curtains and I watch motionless as the digital clock display on my phone flicks silently to 6:00am. I haul my sorry carcass from beneath the sheets and leave Tasha snoring contentedly as I amble to the bathroom. I catch sight of myself in the mirror and would register alarm if I could summon the energy to do so. The bags under my bloodshot eyes sag in shadow and my skin resembles the grey of a short-dated steak on the shelf of a budget supermarket. It's now twelve nights since my brain forgot how to sleep. The frustration and panic of the first five restless nights have long since been replaced by a resigned, zombie-like numbness. I think back over the last eight hours. I must have drifted in and out for short periods, surely?

I cannot say with any certainty what first set in motion this wretched set of circumstances. I had occasionally, I assume like most people, had sleepless nights over the years but nothing of this nature. Whatever the root cause, it had ceased to matter at some point during the third night. The thing had its own legs now. I was not sleeping because I was worried about not sleeping, which was worrying. A never-ending cycle of deafening silences and high-speed stillness.

As I sit and sip at a strong coffee even our pet house rabbit Bovril is giving me a wide berth. His usually expressionless deadpan face eyes me with suspicion from afar, as if enquiring 'what is *with* you?' It's Saturday; at least I don't have the prospect of another unproductive work day ahead of me trying to hide from view my all-too-obvious exhaustion. I make a snap decision to go for a walk in the countryside. Maybe some fresh air in the August sunshine will be of some help.

Eight Months Later:

And so, the day has finally arrived. Friday 1st April 2016. The day I start my adventure: 630 miles, a guidebook (well four of them actually), a pack that's at least 800 times heavier than it should be and a rummy feeling in my gut that mixes excitement and foreboding in equal measure. The sabbatical from work sorted, finances accumulated and the three months spent fielding the same three questions: Why? Is it for charity? And how many of you are going? finally behind me. The answers being: it's complicated, no, and just me. It's not complicated really; in short, so as not to bore you this early on in the proceedings (plenty of time for that later) that walk I went on in the August sunshine ended up changing everything. I discovered by accident that a long walk is far and away the best medicine for insomnia. Cleaning out the old noggin and injecting a slice of much needed physical exertion into my otherwise sloth-like existence. Gradually over the subsequent weeks and months I became an enthusiastic long-distance solitary walker. A hobby that at any time in my life up to that point would have appealed to me slightly less than being captured by Somali pirates. A 37-year-old office worker, who enjoys a tipple and exercises marginally less than the average cheese sandwich. Yet here I was spending my precious weekends exploring the countryside for hours on end, on my tod and loving every minute of it. My sleeping had not returned to what you might class as normality but had improved greatly and reached a level at which I was able to function. And I always slept soundly after a day's walking. So addicted did I become to this blissful self-imposed isolation that one-day walks were soon not enough and I yearned for the freedom of the long-distance trail. The idea was born.

The South West Coast Path is the big daddy of National Trails in the UK. Over 600 miles in length and including some of the toughest terrain these shores have to offer. A challenge that many attempt and fail and that many more take years to complete. So, the obvious choice for a pasty podge-face pushing forty with orienteering skills equal to any cast member of The Only Way is Essex. (Note: this journal is pretty a much dead cert to be an international best seller, read all over the world, so please feel free to insert your own culture's equivalent reference to a reality television show charting the lives of the abominably stupid. Likewise, if you're reading this in 100 years' time or in another galaxy).

The Path starts in Minehead, a Somerset town that is neither the prettiest nor ugliest that I'll encounter on this trip. Along the promenade stands a statue that marks the starting point, a giant pair of cast iron hands holding a map and standing about twelve feet high. My other half, Tasha, and I had driven to the start point early on the morning of the 1st. It takes a very special kind of life partner to agree to be without their dearest love for eight weeks, to stand by and watch as the object of their affections walks off, alone into the sunset like some brave and handsome explorer, perhaps Indiana Jones. So, it's with the deepest admiration and pride that I report to you, dear reader, that Tasha stood strong throughout, somehow holding back her tears. She rallied bravely with jokes about being glad to get rid of me and driving me to Minehead to make sure I'd actually left; that kind of thing. A real trooper.

In addition to Tasha there would be other humans (and the aforementioned rabbit) who would miss me and doubtless yearn for me to return and continue to enrich their otherwise meaningless lives. My family and friends who had all promised, the latter largely with drunken sincerity in the pub, that they would DEFINITELY come and visit me and walk a stretch of the path with me. So I'm absolutely certain this will

3

happen. Worthy of special mention are my parents: My dad (Pops) because he has always loved exploring the countryside and would dearly wish to be taking this journey with me, meaning he would be both a valuable source of advice and an enthusiastic supporter. And my mum because in taking this trip I've condemned her to eight weeks of sleepless worry, certain that she is at any moment day or night about to receive the news that I've fallen down a mineshaft or been murdered by a psychotic Cornish fisherman with a grudge.

After posing by the statue for the obligatory photographs and musing for the first time that 'Blimey, this pack is quite heavy,' Tasha and I walk along the pavement and eventually into some woodland. After 30 minutes or so and an emotional goodbye she turns back and for the first time I'm alone. Curiously Tasha has chosen to retreat at the exact moment we arrive at the bottom of the first steep hill. So, my first twenty minutes alone aren't spent staring in awe at the beauty of my new surroundings or reflecting on how the dream is finally a reality - but rather climbing, red faced and panting up a zig-zagging woodland hillside. When I reach the top, I sling off my pack, collapse onto the floor and reach for my water bottle. Half a mile done, only 629 and a half to go.

1. Somerset & North Devon

Exmoor, Introducing Rolly
and Queen Victoria Toby Jugs

The remaining nine-mile walk to Porlock Weir, once I emerge from the woodland path, is more moorland than coastline. For the most part I'm separated from the sea by several vast windswept Exmoor hills. It somehow has the feel of a first day... a warm up for what is to come, a dipping of the toe. The sun is shining through the gaps in the clouds and there is a strengthening wind as I excitedly stroll onward. The path follows wide farm tracks between fields inhabited with dozing cattle and grazing sheep. As I pass one group of cows I'm sure I hear one say 'Hey girls, get a load of this guy... Look at the size of his backpack, he's not going to get very far.' 'Good luck podgy' another one shouts as I march past.

The path remains flat and easy going over the next few miles before I clamber down a steep slippery valley between two hillsides; the view opens up and I experience the vastness of the sea for the first time. The horizon where water meets skyline, which I'll doubtless become accustomed to over the coming weeks, for now arrests my progress. Wide-eyed and open-mouthed I stare, dumbfounded at the scene.

It's then that I have my first encounter with the wild Exmoor ponies that adorn the North Devon countryside. I spy a group of four trotting enthusiastically at pace towards me. I tell myself there's nothing to worry about as they loom ever closer; just being friendly, I'm sure; merely curious blighters, I'd expect. They come to an abrupt standstill a few feet in front of my petrified frame, wearing expectant expressions. After standing very still avoiding eye contact with the equine natives for a few minutes (maybe seconds), their interest seems to wane and they eventually begin to unenthusiastically graze on the short hillside grass. Clearly I've disappointed them in some way as I assume they were expecting some kind of edible reward for their attentions. Feeling slightly rejected and not very much like a brave explorer, I begin very slowly to edge past them. My heart is still pounding and when they are just out of view I too break into a brief, albeit fractionally less co-ordinated, trot.

Almost immediately thereafter the attractive harbour-side settlement of Porlock Weir comes into view in the distance. For the second time today I'm stopped in my tracks by the breath-taking views of the endless ocean. A short while later during the long descent toward the Weir I pass an eerie area of bare lifeless treetops protruding from the sand, known locally as the dead forest, before a final and somewhat ungraceful haul across a pebbled beach to end the day's walk. My final destination is a room above a restaurant/bar that completely blows my daily budget out of the window before I've even got going. I'm due to meet Pops and my stepmum Jane here later in the evening when they'll treat me to a very welcome hot meal. Even though it has only been a few hours since I said goodbye to Tasha I'm looking forward to seeing them both and telling them all about my first day. They live on Exmoor so I'm hopeful of enjoying their company a few more times during the next week or so of the trip.

The gent at reception is positively thrilled to see a muddy and dishevelled individual with a comically oversized backpack trudging sweatily through his foyer. He duly proceeds with haste to show me to my room, with an expression that whispers tactfully 'Please leave the public area immediately sir.' My room, like the rest of the establishment, is a Hogwarts of Victorian Gothic meets Christmas. Presumably peculiar to my room though is an extensive-to-the-point-ofunnerving collection of Royal-themed trinkets. From Charles and Diana commemorative dining plates to Queen Victoria toby jugs. Even an Andrew and Fergie shot glass. All staring down at me from every corner of the room as I peel off my clothes and collapse onto the creaking four poster.

The evening with Pops and Jane is an enjoyable one spent marvelling at the eccentric décor, scoffing down several elaborately prepared courses and knocking back a good few night caps. Eventually, after arranging to meet up again a bit further down the trail and saying our goodbyes, I retire to my room. I turn off the lights so that the former kings, queens, princes and princesses of England can't see me and take a moment to collect my thoughts. A wave of tipsy excitement washes over me... This is real now, I'm up and running and for the next couple of months it's just me and *the path*. Plus, an oversized, overweight backpack.

Day 2 begins in the April sunshine with a steady ascent through farmland that's littered with excited leaping lambs and their weary mothers. As I pass through the Countess Lovelace's Arches (not as exciting as it may sound) I open my guidebook and glance at the map charting today's 13-mile trek to Lynmouth. The four volumes that make up the official national trail guidebook for the South West Coast Path are exceptionally well written and informative. Each of the four authors does a sterling job of guiding the walker through this mammoth journey. I feel I should get this truth out there from the get-go as I *may* spend much of my time over the next eight weeks swearing at them and wishing a plague upon their households. So, as and when I recount such moments please know with complete clarity that it's I who am the incompetent party. Rolly (my collective name for my guidebooks - a shortened version of one of the authors' first names) is never wrong.

A few hours into a long stretch of dense woodland Rolly advises me that I'm about to see England's smallest Church appear below me through the trees. As I stare down at it from the hillside I scoff and say out loud 'You've got that wrong Rolly old boy. I've seen many a smaller Church than this one in my time. Call yourself a guide? Sloppy.' Needless to say, Culbone Church is of course the smallest in the country. As I continue through the woodland strewn with stunning waterfalls more akin to a tropical rain forest I come to the first, but certainly not the last, path diversion due to erosion or land slips. I start to see glimpses through the tall overhanging trees of the glimmering sea with views across to Wales. The woods are dense and dark and I've not met a single person on the path all day. It strikes me that less hardy souls than myself may by this point be allowing their minds to wander to countless horror movies set in deep dark woods not dissimilar to these. Not I however dear reader. For some reason, I have always felt safe, confident and at home in the woods, even as a child. Just as I think this a man, naked save for a pair of Stag antlers Sellotaped to his head and a long beard made of moss, appears. He beckons me with bloodstained hands to his cave for sweets and cuddles. (Note: that didn't happen.)

When I do eventually meet the first fellow walker of the day, a friendly middle-aged man with eye glasses so thick that his pupils are magnified to alien-like proportions, we exchange pleasantries and swap a few stories. He has been walking the Coast Path most weekends for longer than I've been alive and as his massive eyes glance over my sweaty, red face and oversized backpack a silent judgement is passed; as if to say 'Good luck treacle, you're going to need it.' He then mentions, with some apparent amusement, the Hartland to Bude stretch of the path that's coming up in a week or so. 'I've done it once; never again,' he chuckles. My spirits undampened I continue along the undulating woodland path. There are continued fleeting glimpses of North Devon's dramatic coastline, revealing the scale and challenge of the path sprawling out before me and off into infinity. Eventually after several vicious ascents and descents I arrive, exhausted and aching, at the attractive village of Lynmouth. I buy myself a double cone Mr Whippy with flakes and climb an unjustly steep hill alongside a road to reach my campsite for the night. I set up my tent in a picturesque spot under an oak tree by a flowing river. This successfully ensures I need the loo every twenty minutes throughout the night.

The next morning, after I experience a considerably less comfortable rest than the previous night, Pops and his faithful sheepdog Tiny meet me at the campsite bright and early to accompany me on the first half of the day's 14-mile walk to Combe Martin. Our bellies full of bacon butties and pedigree chum respectively we set off in good spirits. The full majesty of the North Devon coast presents itself to us as the path finally leaves the woodlands behind for the time being. The drama is incredible as we enter the Valley of the Rocks, with winds pushing us onward and pinning us back. The path zigzags through the jagged landscape as families of mountain goats breeze up and down the impossibly steep hillsides with languid ease. Tiny eyes them suspiciously thinking: 'Funny looking sheep, wonder what they taste like.' Eventually I manage to moan about the weight of my backpack to a volume and frequency that causes Pop's resolve to break and he finally 'offers' to carry my tent for me. After numerous climbs and further majestic views we arrive at the foreboding Heddon's Mouth. We descend the vast steep hillside down to sea level and walk half a mile inland to the Hunters Inn pub. Here we meet Jane for a drink after which Pops and Tiny will depart with her.

Well-rested and alone once more my first task is to ascend the other side of Heddon's Mouth. The climb is backbreakingly tough. The weight of my pack causes me to struggle to keep my balance as I sweat and puff my way up the meandering path. At the top, fuzzy with exhaustion, I pull myself along the cliff-side towards the sea and turn the corner. Here I get the pay-off for my heroic climb. I've arrived in an area known as Peter's Rock. I'm startled by the wall of silence that engulfs me. The inward half-moon shape of the rocky landscape some 400 feet up creates a whimsical and slightly surreal scene. As my heart rate slows the angry wind and wild lapping of the sea is replaced by a still serenity and it feels as though I've discovered a secret haven. As though I'm the first person to ever set foot on this turf. I decide there can be no better place to stop for lunch.

As part of my meticulous planning for the trip I'd researched what food supplies I would need with painstaking precision. I subsequently disregarded these findings however and plumped instead for a diet exclusively made up of salami, Mars Bars and individually wrapped mini cheeses. I'm confident that a consistent mixture of protein and sugar will see me through. After devouring my 'Taste the Difference' saucission, sweaty cheese and nougat based confectionary I reluctantly tear myself away from the wonder of Peter's Rock to face the elements once more.

The stunning views continue as I scale the mighty Trentishoe cliff, where I meet a couple out for a day's hike with their ludicrously excited golden Labrador. We chat for a few minutes and they are duly impressed to hear about my 630-mile quest. In fact, so complimentary are they towards my efforts that when I continue on my way I'm internally composing an award acceptance speech, possibly for the 'greatest achievement in the history of mankind award' that I'm sure to win upon crossing the finish line, just after being showered in tickertape by an adoring crowd. 'I'd like to thank my mum and dad for bringing me into this world and teaching me to believe that dreams can come true if I work hard enough... Tasha for being the wind beneath my wings... My 6th Form History teacher Mr Turner for....' I stop in my tracks. There is a public footpath sign ahead of me but no South West Coast Path option on it, no reassuring acorn symbol (the waymarker for all National Trails in the UK). It dawns on me that the sea is very much further away from me than at any other point of today's walk. How long have I been accepting my greatest achievement in the history of mankind award for, without paying attention to where I was going? 20, 30 minutes?

As I spend the next half hour retracing my steps, to eventually find and rejoin the Coast Path and the turning I missed, I take the opportunity to compose an award acceptance speech for the 'moron of the year award' that I'm sure to receive in the unlikely event that I ever make it home. I think back to all the conversations I had before I left with friends and family where I quipped 'It's not like I can get lost, I mean if the sea's on my right-hand side I'm going the right way, hahaha.' How we laughed.

A while later Rolly advises me that I'm approaching the highest point of the entire South West Coast Path. The dramatically-titled Hangman's Hill. It's the second severe and ultimately painful climb of the day. I'm tired and a smidge grumpy as I snail up towards the summit. By the time I reach the top I'm an ungainly panting mess, but it doesn't matter. The payoff is spectacular. A wave of euphoria washes over me as I experience the sensation of feeling like I'm on top of the whole world. As I stand triumphantly astride the cairn I'm almost moved to tears with the sheer exhilaration of it all. The Herculean sea stretches out in front of me and a strong wind revitalises my weary spirit. What's more it's then that I get sight of my final destination for the day as Combe Martin comes into view in the distance.

After spending a few more minutes gazing out to sea and catching my breath on Hangman's, the tiredness begins to kick in again and the long slow descent into Combe Martin drains the last drops of energy from my aching limbs. I have not organised a place to stay for the night and so, when I finally arrive at the main street that runs through the village, I begin to look around for a B&B. After being mercilessly turned away at three separate doorsteps I eventually find a vacancy at a small guesthouse at the end of the road. The two chaps that own and run the establishment are friendly and welcoming to a fault. They usher me in, make me a coffee and we chat about my journey. They advise me that I've just missed a girl who stayed with them who is also walking the entire path on her own. They also note that my backpack is clearly too heavy and that in a few days I've got the Hartland Quay to Bude stretch coming up; 'Rather you than me, best of luck!'

A few hours later, having scoffed down a sub-par burger at a local pub I'm lying in bed listening to an audiobook. I have filled my phone and iPod with a collection of stories and music for the trip. Musically I'm accompanied on this epic voyage by the complete works of Carter the Unstoppable Sex Machine (the greatest band in the history of music… fact), the complete works of Jim Bob (the singer from Carter the Unstoppable Sex Machine's solo moniker) and a selection of tracks from various other artists – all noticeably pre-millennial. In terms of literary works, I have a large number of PG Wodehouse, a selection of crime fiction and all available audiobooks by the author JB Morrison (aka Jim Bob, the singer of the greatest band in musical history; Carter the Unstoppable Sex Machine). I'm currently listening to Coffin Road by the excellent Peter May. As I lay in the dark listening to the narrator traversing the book's themes of memory and sleeplessness I wonder what part, if any, my insomnia will play on this trip. The next thing

I'm aware of is the sound of my alarm going off seven hours later.

Sandy Beaches, Pancakes and Weird Feet

The start of the fourth day is a comparatively flat one with some unpleasant road walking thrown in for good measure. As I begin to get close to the town of Ilfracombe my darkening mood is realised by a road sign in the distance that reads 'Welcome to Hell.' I approach it somewhat apprehensively to discover it actually reads 'Welcome to Hele Bay' but has been tampered with and partially obscured by the overgrown roadside flora. I consider who may have altered the sign and their motives for doing so. It seems a pleasant, sleepy cove, distinctly removed from traditional visions of eternal damnation. I conclude the most probable explanation is bored youths, for whom the day-to-day reality behind descriptions such as pleasant and sleepy would constitute a hellishness of sorts.

I climb up the hill leading out of Hele Bay and into a rabbit warren of footpaths set amongst overgrown woodland. The waymarkers disappear and I'm left to rely on my natural sense of direction if I'm to avoid ending my days on a hillside just outside Hell. I revise my opinion regards the identity of the road sign vandal and imagine now a desperate and disgruntled rambler altering the place name with the intention of warning fellow walkers against entering this forsaken spot. I'll probably discover their decomposing remains at any moment. After a frankly embarrassing amount of time wandering aimlessly I finally pass a clearing in the trees and am greeted by a view of Ilfracombe down below. With a sense of relief, I begin the descent into the attractive seaside resort.

It's impossible to even begin any description of Ilfracombe without talking about Verity. Verity is a 67-foot-high steel and bronze statue that stands at the entrance to the harbour and totally dominates the scene. Created by the artist Damian Hirst; Verity is a heavily pregnant woman wielding a sword and the scales of justice, whilst standing on top of a collection of law books. One side of her naked body has the skin removed to reveal a foetus curled up inside her. Needless to say, she has received a somewhat mixed response from the inhabitants of this small North Devon harbour town. Personally, I love her. Even regardless of her artistic worth; with themes of truth and justice – like a modern, realist Statue of Liberty - I think she's beautiful. But then I don't have to live with her. If you live in Ilfracombe and don't like Verity - it's kind of impossible to avoid her.

Having rested at the feet of the controversial young lady to consume my meat, cheese and chocolate based daily rations, I'm now weaving my way through the streets of Ilfracombe and up the hill on the other side. The sun is now shining brightly and as the path gets more interesting and challenging the views in either direction are stunning. I stop and chat to a chap who I'll call Tony. Tony isn't actually his name, but he looks like a Tony. Tony is wearing camouflage trousers and some sort of military survival sleeveless jacket with at least 900 pockets in the front. Every pocket appears to be full; with what, I don't ask. He can only be about 40 and if I had to guess I would say his attire is not representative of his profession in any factual sense. Despite a slightly intimidating first appearance Tony seems to be a lovely guy who holidays in Ilfracombe every year to walk nearby sections of the Coast Path. This is his first year doing so without his beloved dog, who he tells me sadly passed away a few months ago. After a few minutes, we part ways and wish each other well. A minute or so down the path I turn around to look at the view and see

Tony standing watching me in the spot where I left him, staring intently at me with arms folded and a stony straight face. I decide he's probably just soaking up the view as well so I give him a little wave and keep going. After another minute, I glance behind me a second time and Tony is still there, arms folded, legs apart, watching me as I walk away. I move on swiftly and don't turn around at any point during the next half hour.

My feet are starting to scream at me by the time I reach the beautiful Lee Bay. The weight of my pack, as well as giving me an increasingly unpleasant rash on my shoulders is causing the pressure points on my feet to start to hurt during the last few miles of each day. I'm confident my feet will man up over time and after consulting Rolly I see that the day after tomorrow's walk is nearly all on the flat tarmac as I make my way around the first estuary of the trip. This news buoys my spirits as I assume it will be practically like a day off; no hills and a chance for the feet to recover.

I spend a short while in Lee Bay watching the sea lapping at the rocky shoreline as noisy gulls swoop from cliff to cliff. Then there is a steep climb out of the bay along the roadside followed by a short stretch containing many steeper, stepped climbs that leave me utterly exhausted by the time I reach the cheerfully named Morte Point. Morte Point, like Hangman's Hill the previous day is an important landmark early on in this journey. It's the point at which I turn the first major corner. I'm no longer looking out across the Bristol Channel to Wales. Although I won't be officially looking at the Atlantic Ocean for a few days yet it feels like a big moment and I get my first proper sight of Lundy Island. It's also a notorious spot historically for shipwrecks (hence the name) and will have been the last sight witnessed by numerous unlucky folk in years gone by. I consider the possibility of it being the last sight I witness as I'm unsure if my feet can take me any further. It's then that I catch sight of my destination for the day; Woolacombe. The sight causes me to double take as no sooner have I turned the corner at Morte Point when the rocky rugged cliffs are replaced by a vast yellow sandy beach. Littered with hundreds of surfers, the scene is surreal, almost absurd. The sun is beating down on the sparkling blue sea and I wonder how I've gone from North Devon in April to the California sunshine in the space of five minutes.

Woolacombe is a small surfer village full of trendy surf 'n' turf restaurants and bars as well as various surf related shops. After wandering around taking it all in for a while I stop at one of the bars, order an ale with a plate of fish and chips and sit contentedly, looking out across the beach. I end up remaining in this picturesque spot for the evening and watch a beautiful sunset with a warm tipsy glow.

The next morning I'm sat in an American Diner eating pancakes swimming in maple syrup for breakfast. The walls are adorned with pictures of Betty Boop, James Dean, Mickey Mouse and Marilyn Monroe. A vintage jukebox is pumping out Beach Boys tunes and an old 1950s surfing video is playing on a TV screen in the corner. To say that the owners of the B&B I stayed at last night are proud of their novelty retro diner would be something of an understatement. As they bop from table to table pouring out fresh coffee the whole scene has the feel of a long running Las Vegas show where the performance is played out each and every morning of the year, each time with the same enthusiasm and excitement. It's impossible not to enjoy it.

After the heaviest breakfast in living memory I saunter down to the beach to begin the 15-mile trek to Braunton. I meet Pops, Jane and Tiny on the beach for what will probably be the last time of the journey; I've been walking further away from their homestead for a few days now and after today will be out of range. They'll walk the first hour along the sands with me before heading back. We discuss all the adventures that still lie ahead of me as the bright sun warms the sand beneath our feet and scores of surfers appear from VW camper vans in every imaginable colour scheme to take up residence amongst the lapping waves once more.

When the time comes for them to turn back I feel a pang of loneliness with the realisation that I'm now on my own for real. I have no doubt there will be a few other visits from friends and family during the course of the journey, but for a while at least it's just me, Rolly and the endless ocean. I push on to Baggy Point where I catch sight of a buzzard for the first time. I stand watching as the graceful and majestic bird glides overhead surveying the land beneath it, with views of Lundy Island ever-present in the background. Soon after this I cross my second beach of the day at Croyde and by the time I reach the third of the day at Saunton Sands the novelty of walking on loose sand in heavy boots whilst lugging the cursed backpack has all but evaporated. To compound matters further I must then cross a golf course.

Whilst I would not yet call myself an experienced long-distance walker I have 'trod the trail' for long enough to have developed a potent loathing for the sport of golf and all who partake of it. Although you might not know it golfers and walkers are, to my mind, natural enemies. They may move amongst each other in polite society as if given the chance they would not inject each other with a deadly killer virus or set fire to each other's eyeballs. But this is merely a mask worn by way of concession, so as not to bring about the end of the civilised world. Out here, on the battlefield, away from the muggles, anything goes.

The walker's argument is thus: I'm out here, in the rugged, isolated beauty of nature. I'm miles from anywhere and in a state of bliss only understood by the fellow cagouled rambler of the species and then 'Bang!' Some jive turkey plonks a giant golf course where my path should be. The wonder of nature is replaced by manicured lawns, gravel tracks and signs warning me of the dangers I'm about to face by having the temerity to enter here. Then when I try and negotiate my way through this prissy wasteland I'm met by the tuts of the argyle sweater brigade who look at me as though I'm Stig of the Dump dirtying up their precious course. As for the golfer's argument... Well, who cares? They are evil people and I will not indulge their irrational views.

True to form I'm lost shortly after entering the course. Rolly is as much help as a guide dog's cataract and I'm eventually shown the way back to the path by a passive-aggressive American lady, aged somewhere between 300 and 400 years old, with leather skin and a luminous pink baseball cap. I've clearly interrupted her game and her assistance is fuelled by a desire to be rid of me rather than by any semblance of kindness. After calming the nerves, I reach Braunton Burrows Nature Reserve. The Burrows is of historical significance primarily because it was used during the Second World War as a training ground for the Normandy landings. It's also of ecological importance as it's the largest area of sand dunes in the country. I cannot lie to you, however: none of these points of interest are at the forefront of my mind as I slump onwards in the afternoon sunshine; my feet have given up the ghost entirely. Every step is fresh agony and the pack on my back now feels like a giant sack of spanners. I stop and peel off the boots and socks for a moment to let my feet take a breather. I'm struck by their resemblance to skinless raw chicken.

After a sustained period of feeling sorry for myself I clamber to my feet and hobble onwards. A bounding wiry man of pensionable age sidles up beside me in sandals and shorts carrying a well-used and noticeably small rucksack. I won't repeat in full our ensuing conversation, but in summary I'm advised: I'm carrying too much stuff; I look terrible and exhausted, I'm not going to fair well on the Hartland to Bude stretch; and that I ought to be aiming for closer to 20 miles a day if I'm *really* wanting to complete the entire Coast Path. After delivering this motivational speech he strides off into the distance. For the first time, I think I can see things from the golfer's perspective.

Sometime later I arrive, emotionally and physically deflated, in Braunton. I haven't booked anywhere to sleep and so I knock on the doors of each of the village's three B&B's. I'm turned away by each one. I wander back down the path out of Braunton to see if I can spot any potential places to pitch the tent, but I'm really in the wrong place to try out wild camping for the first time. The walk into Braunton is along the River Caen and offers no obvious camping options. Likewise in the other direction out of Braunton – where Rolly advises me that the path continues along the riverside to the estuary that makes up tomorrow's walk. Thankfully I'm too tired to panic or even muster annoyance and so after some deliberation I decide on the course of action I must take. I'll get a bus to nearby Barnstaple, stay the night in a hotel (which I should be able to manage without booking ahead in a town of that size) and then catch the bus back here tomorrow morning to then walk back to Barnstaple as part of tomorrows leg. A winning end to a winning day.

On the bus journey over I get talking to a nice chap who is on his way to Switzerland on holiday. He advises me which hotels I should try when I get to Barnstaple and even recommends a pub for dinner. This conversation perks me up a bit and when I arrive in Barnstaple, after wishing him well on his travels, I book into the nearest available hotel. I dump my stuff and head straight for the aforementioned pub where I eat chips and drink beer until they eventually ask me to leave.

Boring Estuaries, Non-Existent Castles
and Hartland to Bude

After arriving back in Braunton and rejoining the path the next day I'm feeling confident about the walk ahead. Since having my pride dented slightly by old wiry sandal man back at Braunton Burrows, I've decided to take advantage of the flat easy walk around the estuary and make some time up by extending the distance for the day to 23 miles. It's a bold move given the state of my feet but I figure it's mainly tarmac and gravel paths so how hard can it be?

A few hours later I'm sat huddled under a tree in the pouring rain at Fremington staring down at my angry purple feet and silently cursing my own stupidity. The rain has been constant and driving all day and I'm nowhere near half distance yet. Having negotiated Barnstaple and many a busy road to get to this point I'm thoroughly fed up of flat tarmac paths already. I soldier on, soaked to the bone and muttering crazed exclamations of discomfort with every step.

When I arrive at the bridge that crosses the estuary at Bideford sometime later I decide to stop in a pub for a late lunch. I sit with my feet elevated, pointing at a roaring open fire, nursing an ale and nibbling tentatively at the sorriest looking cheese sandwich I've ever seen. I consider phoning my mum and crying at her… but ultimately decide this wouldn't be a very becoming move for a 37-year-old Indiana Jones-type brave explorer.

I pass through Bideford and the picturesque village of Appledore with its narrow, cobbled streets and colourful terraced cottages. Eventually I reach Northam Burrows from where, Rolly advises me, it's a gentle stroll to my final destination for the day; the brilliantly named Westward Ho! I'm still feeling sorry for myself as I begin the long walk across the burrows and the mushy purple splats where my feet used to be are still causing me much discomfort. I distract myself by in turns cursing Rolly's chipper optimism and contemplating how other place names would sound with the addition of an exclamation mark. *Bognor Regis! Swindon! Bath Spa!*

I can just see Westward Ho! in the far distance when the driving rain turns into a full-scale hailstorm. A major feature of Northam Burrows is that it's a wide-open expanse. No trees, no shelter. I stand defeated, drenched, feet throbbing, weighed down by my backpack as thousands of miniature balls of ice pelt me from every angle at breakneck speed. It's a low point.

Later that evening, having booked a room above a pub along the Westward Ho! seafront and taken a long hot bath, I wander out to stare at the sea. It's angry. The waves violently crash against and topple over the promenade wall as the wind howls and the rain falls once more. It's breathtakingly beautiful and the rigmarole of the day is instantly forgotten. It's stiff upper lip time... I'm on a journey, and the journey must go on. The flat, dull paths of the estuary are behind me and tomorrow's hike to Clovelly promises a triumphant return to form.

After an inexplicably early start due to an untimely sleepless night (which I've chosen to ignore) my spirits are sky high mid-way through the next morning. I'm walking an undulating hillside path in a blustery wind, way above the still raging waves. Dramatic far-reaching views and a sense of total isolation leave me almost euphoric in light of the last 24 hours. I take a detour down onto the beach and the sea, suddenly conscious that I've barely touched the surface of my constant companion over the last week. I strip my wounded feet bare and tentatively dip my toes in the ice-cold, angry ocean. I enjoy a brief second before the cold truly penetrates where I imagine that there is a bond between the sea and I, an understanding, a connection that renders the icy water warm and pleasant against my skin. Something truly unique and spiritual.

I then spend the next five minutes doing Frankie Howerd impressions; ooh-erring all over the shop as the cold mercilessly floods my insides. 'Up yours, the Sea' I cry as I clumsily leap from rock to rock back to my abandoned boots and socks. I climb back up to the path and consult with Rolly. He advises me that I'll shortly be passing Peppercombe Castle. I stride on enthusiastically, looking all about me for the aforementioned monument as I go. An hour later I finally conclude that Peppercombe Castle does not exist. Rolly has cracked. The isolation of the long-distance trek has left his anthropomorphised pages in a state of terminal gobbledygook. Poor fellow. Thank goodness he has a sane companion to look after him.

I stop for lunch at Buck Mills and make an important culinary decision. It's time to let the individually wrapped mini cheeses go. Big words I know but hear me out. They are sweaty. Increasingly so. As I walk gallantly onwards through this breath-taking coastline I do so amidst a potent cloud of smelly cheese. No more. If cured meat products and nougat based confectionary items aren't all I need to see me through the next 500 plus miles, then I simply don't know what I'm talking about.

No more than an hour into the afternoon and the walking is still excellent. I'm seeing enticing glimpses of the beautiful Clovelly getting ever closer through the trees as the path becomes shrouded in woodland once more. I'm slowing down however as, right on schedule, my feet are starting to throb. I'm hobbling at less than a mile an hour as I reach the start of Hobby Drive; a broad track that will lead me into Clovelly. The woodland becomes thick and dense for the final few miles of the day's walk.

It strikes me, not for the first time on this trip, how much rubbish there is strewn about me. I cannot fathom the mindset of people that would bring a packed lunch out to the middle of the countryside and then just leave all their crap behind. Beer cans, fag butts, crisp packets and cola bottles, littering the beautiful wilderness. It just doesn't make sense to me... Either you're the type of person that drops litter and doesn't care about anything other than yourself or you're the type of person who goes for a long walk in the countryside. How can anyone be both? That's what is most distressing about it all I think. I become increasingly angry the more I notice and am muttering profanities under my breath. I won't repeat them as if you are reading this there is, I estimate, a one-in-five chance that you are my grandmother (Hi Grandma) and I will not swear in front of my grandmother for someone as worthless as a litterbug.

As I arrive in Clovelly the isolation of the walk is replaced by a coachload of tourists. Here to marvel at the undoubted beauty of this tiny unspoilt village sticking out into the sea. The village is essentially one very steep cobbled street running down to a small harbour. The street is adorned on either side by picture-postcard cottages with crooked beams and hobbit front doors. As I wade through the small crowd to the pub where I'm staying, I'm thankful not to be here a month later in full summer season. I find my way to the pub and am greeted by the landlady who shows me to my room. She is a friendly woman whose voice rasps with the memory of a thousand cigarettes. As has become customary I've booked the cheapest room available, with shared bathroom and single bed. However, the landlady advises that I've been upgraded for free as there is nobody else booked in tonight and I now have a double bed with en-suite. Result.

Later that evening I'm sitting in the pub with a plate of chips and a pint. I phone Tasha, my folks and my brother Mark and look over my notes from the first week. It dawns on me that I've now walked 100 miles. A milestone moment only slightly tainted by the thought of another 530 miles carrying that backpack and listening to my screaming feet.

After a decent night's sleep, I'm chomping on some Weetabix when an idea hits me. I remember having a tube of ibuprofen gel in the darkest recesses of my pack. I finish my breakfast and return to my room to pack up before setting off for the day. I find the tube of gel and proceed to cover my feet in it. I generously rub on about four layers then decide I may as well use the entire tube. It's slightly past its use-by date but I assume this to be of no concern. I don the kit and say my thankyou to the ashen landlady as I pass her wheezing on a gasper by the pub's front door. I'm about halfway back up the hill out of Clovelly when my error of judgement becomes apparent. My feet have gone completely numb. I also simultaneously lose some degree of spatial awareness as the lack of any sensation (other than a faint tingling) in my feet leaves me unable to judge where the ground is. I resemble an astronaut walking on the surface of the moon as I attempt to carry on up the hill. When I reach the top I waste most of the day's water supply washing my feet. Initially this makes little difference but the feeling eventually begins to return as I ludicrously push on, feeling like Mr Soft from the Softmints TV ad.

After a long stretch of ancient woodland, I reach open farmland and a clifftop path. Here I meet the saddest horse in the world. He ambles over to me and walks, stony-faced, alongside me for some distance. I don't have the vocabulary required to describe to you how sad this horse looks so you'll need to take my word for it. At the next stile, we say an emotional goodbye and I leave him with some words of much needed encouragement. I can only hope he takes them on board and turns his life around. The sun is out and the temperature warm, but the sea is still anything but calm below me. The going is getting tougher as the day wears on with increasingly steep descents down to sea level and ascents back up to the cliff edge again. My pack is weighing heavy on my back although, and I only dare whisper it, I do sense a toughening up in that regard. I think I'm slowly starting to get used to the weight. The same can't be said for my feet however and, the gel having now completely worn off, they are aching to buggery once again by the time I stop for lunch. As I'm chowing down on the old salami and Mars combo the second bright idea of the day, vis-à-vis the much aforementioned feet, occurs. Socks. I have three pairs of extra thick walking socks with me; why am I only wearing one of them at a time?

A more pessimistic fellow than yours truly may allow himself to dwell on how blindingly obvious this potential solution seems. An even more down in the mouth chap might border on despair that it had taken him this long, and an entire tube of expired ibuprofen gel, to grasp it. Not I. It's with mounting excitement that I set off after lunch adorned in additional socks. The difference is positive and immediate, though by no means total. The cushioning of the pressure points turns down the pain a couple of notches. Enough though, to understand that padding is the answer. Huzzah!

The remaining miles to Hartland are eventful. Firstly, I stumble upon a valley full of bluebells. The first I've seen this year. As well as being a beautiful sight to behold this gives me an amazing sense of progression. I'll watch the seasons change during this walk. The very tail end of winter was still in evidence on the high desolate clifftops of Exmoor. Spring is now in the air and I may even see the first signs of summer before I reach Poole Harbour. This could turn out to be wishful thinking but it's pleasing nonetheless, to be reminded of the enormity of walking 630 miles in one go. I then come across a military radar; a giant futuristic mushroom perched on a clifftop, completely at odds with the natural beauty surrounding it. It seems I'm being regularly reminded of this coastline's important military connections. Historically interesting but, thus far, visually depressive.

Everything gets a bit Tolkien as I near Hartland Quay. Jagged rocks protrude from the rich green landscape as the sea reaches fever pitch hundreds of feet below. My hotel for the evening is the only building in view for miles around, perched right out amongst the raging waves. Hartland is the point where the Atlantic Ocean officially meets the Bristol Channel and this makes for all year-round stormy drama. My room, which I've again acquired on the cheap as the hotel's boiler is down, has a huge bay window facing the sea. After dining in the excellent pub attached to the hotel (and having a drink with a father and son in the bar who are walking a three day stretch of the Coast Path) I retire to my room, move an armchair in front of the window and sit and watch the oceans endlessly collide until it's too dark to do so. My heart is full.

Behold the day is upon us. Hartland to Bude. A growing sense of foreboding engulfs me over my Weetabix as I think back on all the warnings I've received regards today's 15-mile hike into Bude and the county of Cornwall. I peruse a leaflet on local walks picked up in the hotel foyer as I sit at the breakfast table. For the walk along the coast to Bude it says 'not for the faint-hearted' and advises '8-9 hours' walking time. Gulp. Rolly describes the day's trek as 'severe' and advises me I'll pass no towns or villages until Bude. Gulp. I feel as though I'm heading off into battle.

Due to the lack of shops I've not been able to acquire any padding for the feet and so I've gone the whole hog and am wearing all three pairs of walking socks. I cannot move my toes but this feels like a three-socker of a day. Feeling as ready as I'll ever be I head off with the waves still crashing below. After an initial climb, out of the Quay, the path is winding but not immensely difficult. Then I hit an area called Speakes Mill Mouth and the day really gets going. A steep climb and descent then immediate climb up again sets the tone for the rest of the day. Not only in terms of difficulty though, as what all those folks who warned me about today didn't think to mention is how utterly spectacular this walk is. Speakes Mill gives me the first of the day's amazing views, as well as a pair of stunning waterfalls.

Further steep climbs and descents at Swansford Hill and Welcombe Mouth offer similar challenge and similar reward. They are interspersed with cliff edge stretches and a number of small diversions due to erosion. Eventually, already exhausted, I come across a tiny hut positioned on a hillside, in total isolation. Rolly duly advises that this is the bolthole of one Ronald Duncan, a playwright and poet who used the hut as a means of escape and inspiration to get the creative juices flowing. A little tentatively, I open the door and venture inside. There are a small table and chair in an otherwise bare room, save for examples of Duncan's works adorning the walls. On the table is a large bottle of water as well as a pen and an open book. A note says I'm welcome to take a drink and write something in the book before I leave. I do both and then take five minutes to read some of the comments left by other walkers over the months and years. All previous comments are emotional outpourings at the sheer beauty of this place and of the writer's works. This makes me feel guilty and I cross out my joke complaining at the lack of parking and toilet facilities and replace it with an acceptable platitude.

Another steep descent awaits immediately upon leaving the hut. This one is Marshlands Mouth and at the footbridge that crosses a stream at the bottom I pass a wooden sign that says Kernow Cornwall. North Devon is behind me, North Cornwall awaits. Under different circumstances this may be an emotional moment for me… but I'm knackered and all too aware of what still awaits me, so I plough onwards.

Yet more steep climbs at Litter Mouth, Cornakey Cliff, Yeol Mouth and the back-breaking Henna Cliff follow. The views back into North Devon are simply breath-taking. I stop for a late lunch at the top of Henna Cliff where I meet the father and son that I'd had a drink with the previous night. I'm ashamed to say I'm slightly pleased to note that they are also panting, red-faced and sweaty. We chat for a few minutes – they took a taxi out to Bude this morning and are walking back to the hotel, so are walking in the opposite direction to myself. They advise me that I've broken the back of the walk and will be in Bude before too long. This lifts me and I muster the strength to carry on.

A short while later I pass a satellite tracking station which fences off some of the most ludicrously large satellite dishes I've ever seen. It's all bit space station. To be honest with you dear reader, it all goes a bit blurry at this point. My feet, which up until now have been fairly quiet thanks to the additional sock-age, wave the white flag and die a sudden death. I'm left to essentially crawl for the remaining miles into Bude. There are a few more steep climbs to negotiate and then a long final descent into the popular surfing hotspot. The sun is beating down on my sweaty mess of a body as it has been all day.

I make my way to the campsite I'm booked into, where I make a decision. I will take a day off tomorrow and book a room in a B&B for tomorrow night. I'm running low on food supplies and need to purchase some proper foot padding, insoles or suchlike. Buoyed by this decision and having set up my tent I make my way to a nearby pub for dinner. As I sit eating I contemplate the day behind me. I feel as though a physical milestone has been reached today. Although I'm more tired than I've been at any point up until now, it's somehow a good tired.

2. North Cornwall

Camelot, the Turquoise Sea and Canadian Dentists

After an uncomfortable night under the canvas I spend the morning wandering Bude in search of supplies. I buy padded insoles and various assorted plasters for the poor old feet as well as stocking up on lunches. Replenishing the Mars Bars proves of no difficulty, but the salami search is less fruitful. In the end, I'm reduced to a multi-pack of a popular brand of processed snacking sausages. The *horror*. I also find a launderette to give my clothes a desperately needed wash. My by-now-pretty-fruity undergarments practically leap into the machine and select the appropriate spin cycle without any human assistance. I book a room at a pub around lunchtime, dump my stuff and wander down to the beach. Here I spend the afternoon basically watching the clock and wishing I was back on the trail. I honestly thought I'd revel in a day off; a good rest, maybe catch a movie, read a book or whatever. The reality is that I'm bored, twitchy and ultimately desperate to get going again. Eventually I sulk my way back to the pub for an evening meal and an early night.

By the time the 6am alarm sounds on my phone the next morning I'm already up, dressed, breakfasted and heading for the door. My feet are double-socked, plastered up and sitting snuggly atop a thick pair of cushioned insoles. I stride down to the beach to rejoin the path like a man possessed, consumed by the need to be back on the trail. The sun is already shining brightly and the skies are a clear brilliant blue. After climbing out of Bude I'm walking along a gently undulating grassy hilltop path. Crowds of gulls and crows are gracefully acting out a complex display of flying prowess above me. Swooping and rising with effortless speed and accuracy as the calm, eternal sea glitters and sparkles beneath.

I walk past a striking monument standing proud and isolated on the hilltop. I consult Rolly to discover it's a 19th century storm tower also known as the Tower of the Winds. The gentle grassy slopes continue until I reach the sand dunes of Widemouth bay, where the surfers again pepper the early morning sea. I cannot pretend that I haven't to some extent lost track of what day it is already, but I'm fairly certain it's a weekday. I wonder if none of the surfers that have filled the beaches since Woolacombe have got jobs to go to? I mean I'm obviously one to talk... maybe they're all on sabbatical too. A section of steep road walking follows the dunes as I ascend to the clifftop once more.

I meet a couple of farmers working on some fencing along the cliff edge. We chat for a while and I tell them about my trip. They have the thickest Cornish accents I've ever heard and in between each sentence I speak the younger of them seems to exclaim 'Diddah?' whilst the elder quietly mutters what sounds like 'Issoo?' in unison behind him.

'I got three months booked off work'

'Diddah?'

'Issoo?'

'Yes, and I'm walking the whole Coast Path round to Poole harbour.'

'Diddah!?'

'Issoo?'

They tell me about a decent pub at my day's final destination of Crackington Haven and, after taking a bit of gentle mocking at the size of my backpack, we say our goodbyes. I have never felt less like a brave explorer and more like an office worker from the city on vacation in my entire life.

Straight away the path becomes more challenging. A series of very steep drops and climbs to rival anything from the previous stretch follow in quick succession. I eventually stop for lunch when I arrive at the staggeringly beautiful Millook valley. I sit on the rocky beach between the majestic jagged cliff faces and devour my slightly less majestic meaty rations. I watch a bird of prey, I think a kestrel, behind and above me hovering as though frozen in time before suddenly dropping like an arrow from the sky. Way up above me a tiny rodent of some description is having a very bad day.

Back on the cliff edge after a few more tough climbs the views are mesmerising. Stretching back to Hartland in one direction and on to Tintagel in the other. I spot a sleeping bag on the path in front of me. It's clearly new and clean and I assume it's fallen off someone's pack without them noticing. As I have no idea which direction they will have been walking in, I follow the walkers' unspoken code of practice and carry it with me to the next style, where I hang it from a fence post in plain sight. About five minutes later I'm climbing a steep grassy hillside and I pass two elderly ladies out walking. They advise me that Crackington Haven is only another 30 minutes away and this puts a spring in the old step.

A further 20 minutes on and I'm daydreaming about seals. I'm now entering the 100 miles or so of the path where I'm advised I'm most likely to catch sight of them. I'm picturing their sweet blubbery faces when I hear a distant call that sounds like 'Coowweee.' I look all around me but see nothing. I hear the call again and then, after a few confused seconds, a figure comes into view over the crest of the hill behind me. As the figure approaches I realise it's one of the ladies I passed 20 minutes ago, and that she is waving the sleeping bag I found earlier above her head, slightly frantically.

'Hello, I think you dropped this.' She is sweating and panting and has clearly spent the last 20 minutes chasing me along the path.

'Er, no. I saw that but it's not mine.' She is visibly crestfallen and I instantly think that the gentlemanly reaction would have been to have just said it's mine and thanked her for her kindness. Feeling guilty I say I'll take it from her and hand it in at the pub in Crackington. Partially appeased she slumps off and I begin the descent into the now clearly visible final destination.

Once I arrive I book a room at the Coombe Barton pub that dominates this small and beautiful spot, hand in the sleeping bag and order a bottle of ale. I sit on a bench outside the pub watching the gently crashing waves in the bright sunshine and think that life really doesn't get much better than this. Later that evening in the pub I chat to the barman and a few of the locals. I discover that there is a young German guy staying here who is also walking the whole path and just a few days ago a girl on her own doing the same thing. I wonder if this is the same girl the owners of the guesthouse back in Combe Martin mentioned. It's a strange thought. That I'm sharing this path and this journey with other solitary souls who are, to some extent, experiencing the same adventure as me. I'm undecided as to whether this is comforting or nauseating. The journey seems so personal to me, and yet, to know there are others, maybe seeking the same things for similar reasons, does somehow make me feel part of something bigger. Or maybe I've just had a few too many.

The next morning I'm munching on some cornflakes... the pub doesn't have Weetabix, much to my disgust. The only other guest up at 7am is a chap maybe in his 70s who is using the bar phone. 'Yes, hello there. I wonder if you might have a room available for tonight? I'm walking this confounded path you see.' He is a slight, bald and bespectacled gentleman with the booming baritone of Brian Blessed. After successfully securing a room with whoever is on the other end of the line he seats himself in the chair opposite to me and begins tucking into a plate of scrambled eggs.

'Are you walking the Coast Path as well?' I say.

'Oh, splendid a fellow journeyman?' he booms, looking up at me. We get chatting and it transpires he is walking as far as Penzance. He is a retired school teacher who has walked the entire path in separate sections several times over but never in one go. He is impressed at my efforts thus far and his enthusiasm and excitement are utterly infectious. He gives me a ten-minute talk on a product called Compeed, which will apparently sort out all my foot based problems. Somewhere during the seventh or eighth minute of this lecture, which includes a visual demonstration, I wonder briefly if he is an undercover Compeed salesman, or major shareholder, but I eventually agree to purchase some when I next stop for supplies. My destination for the day is Tintagel whilst his is somewhat further along the path. He encourages me to stay at a particular castle-themed hotel tonight. 'It's quite the experience I assure you. Especially if you're fortunate enough to run into the proprietor.' He is wearing a mischievous look on his face that unnerves me but I agree to take his advice as I've not booked anywhere as yet.

The path rises steeply out of Crackington in the hot, hazy sunshine. It continues to rise and fall in the vein of the last few days as it clings to the rocky hillsides. The sea has changed colour to a brilliant turquoise that gives an almost Mediterranean feel to the walk. I stop, exhausted, at the top of a cliff somewhere past Little Strand beach. The views in the bright sunlight are simply outstanding as I lie red-faced and panting having slung off the blasted pack. My Compeed-loving companion from breakfast appears over the crest of the hill. 'Easier than Bude though, eh?' he proclaims as he smiles down at me. He is astonished at the size of my backpack and encourages me to ditch the tent immediately. As he bounds off cheerfully, at a pace I can barely fathom, I contemplate his suggestion. I've only camped a few times so far and didn't exactly enjoy it. On top of this the accommodation so far has been a lot cheaper than I was expecting, as I'm still out of season. Could I actually lose the tent and sleeping bag, and the weight that comes with it?

By the time I reach the highest cliff in Cornwall; cryptically named High Cliff, my breakfast companion and I have passed each other several more times. Whilst I maintain the steady dependable pace of an overweight tortoise with a heart condition he appears to be walking at breakneck speed and then needing to stop and rest at regular intervals. Even though I've only just met the man this erratic yet determined walking style seems to perfectly sum up his personality. I eventually arrive in the pleasant village of Boscastle, where I stop for lunch in the National Trust café.

The breath-taking views, clear blue skies, turquoise seas and tough climbs all continue into the afternoon. Repeatedly descending into beautiful rocky valleys and climbing relentlessly out of them, way up high above the waves. The drops from the cliff edge to the ocean are sheer here, noticeably more so than recently. There is a jagged edge to the tranquil summer-like scene. As I approach Tintagel I'm tired and the feet are aching, but my observations from the last few days are definitely ringing true; this is starting to get easier. I bravely vow to keep hold of the tent for now.

Tintagel is said to be the home of King Arthur and the Knights of the Round Table. As I arrive the streets are heaving with tourists, weaving in and out of the endless Camelot-themed trinket shops selling magical crystals, Lancelot tea towels and plastic swords. I join the crowds to walk around the castle ruins before deciding to try and locate the hotel my breakfast companion recommended to me earlier that day. This doesn't prove to be difficult as it turns out to be the giant Victorian faux medieval castle building I passed when I left the path to climb into Tintagel. Its prominent position means it has actually been in view for the last day and a half of walking.

It's difficult to know where to start when attempting to describe this bold and memorable accommodation. As you walk through the giant doorway the first thing that hits you is that the interior stone walls are painted in a striking gold. They are also adorned with framed photographs, in which the same sharply dressed, cleanly shaven, hairspray-laden man can be seen shaking hands with a variety of Hollywood celebrities. There is also a portrait shot of the aforementioned chap in seductive soft focus, staring down at you as you wait at reception. The effect is gloriously eccentric and I instantly want to explore the whole building. I'm of course in the budget room, which is essentially a broom cupboard overlooking the car park, but it's cheap and well worth it to stay in such a grand abode.

After I've showered and unpacked a few things a terrifying realisation hits me. Where is Rolly? Usually rolled up and sitting tatty and used in the front pocket of my bag, he's now nowhere to be found. I have no idea when I last consulted him so I get dressed and take a wander around the hotel and grounds, trying to retrace my steps. As I'm doing so I get the chance to take in the decor of this imposing structure. Think 'What if Laurence Llewelyn-Bowen moved into Buckingham Palace and redecorated?' And you'd not be far wrong. An hour or so later after walking all the way back down to the path, via the village centre, I'm forced to concede defeat. I've not met anyone else walking the path who is using the guidebooks, but it has become habitual for me and I'll feel a bit lost without it. There are only a couple of days left before I switch to the second guidebook in the series anyway; a new Rolly. King Rolly is dead, long live King Rolly.

A few hours later I'm tucking into a pasta dinner in the elaborately decked out hotel restaurant when the man in all the photographs wanders in carrying a small child. He's wearing a white linen suit with the sleeves pushed up, like a character from Miami Vice. He proceeds to do the rounds, chatting to a selection of guests as they eat their meals. I wonder if the other diners are as perplexed at this as I am. 'So, please do tell me what you think of my humble abode' he says as he chats to an American couple sat behind me as I silently prey that he'll pass me by. I needn't have worried, he takes one look at me sitting alone, slurping tagliatelle in my faded Carter USM t-shirt and baggy shorts, gives a curt smile that gets nowhere near his eyes and moves swiftly on.

Later that evening I'm lying in bed chatting to my brother on the phone, having already called Tasha and the folks. I tell him about the hotel and its suave owner and he updates me on events back in the real world. It's the first time we've spoken at length since I started the trip and it's good to describe my larger-than-life lodgings to someone who shares my sense of humour. It's a strange by-product of being on your own on a trip like this. I probably wouldn't have seen my brother in the previous two weeks had I not been walking the Coast Path, and yet talking to him now I'm conscious of how much I miss him. It's the distance I suppose.

The walk to Port Isaac the following day is a shorter but more challenging one. This is all I can remember from Rolly's description as I set off without him bright and early. A slightly sobering thought, as I don't recall the previous few days being particularly unchallenging. The going is initially easy as I steadily climb out of Tintagel. There are some very pleasant hedge-enclosed sections where I'm serenaded by multiple birdsongs in the bright early morning breeze. Then things get tougher very quickly with a series of steep descents down to sea level and sharp climbs back of up to 400ft.

As ever with this section the views at the peak of each climb are sensational. The beautiful rugged cliffs set against the turquoise (I might be using that word too much?) water and rich blue skies peppered (and that one?) with gulls patrolling diligently. At the top of Dennis Point I stop to watch a peregrine flying by. I've never seen one before and the sight, like the buzzards and kestrels I've encountered already on this trip, is jaw-dropping. It's gliding through the air and then suddenly diving at breakneck speed, arrow shaped, towards the ground before pulling up at the last moment. I can't see anything that it could be hunting and so assume it's merely playing. I'm utterly transfixed by it until, eventually, it passes from view.

A little further along I pass a young chap with walking poles who holds a gate open for me.

'How far are you going?' I ask, by now used to receiving the adoration of strangers when they hear I'm walking the entire Coast Path.

'John O'Groats' he says.

I'm instantly in awe and we chat for a few minutes about the journey he has ahead of him. South West Coast Path? Child's play. A bit further still and I'm staring slack jawed once again, this time at the stunning views from the top of Bounds Cliff. It's difficult to imagine the path maintaining this level of beauty for the next six weeks and it crosses my mind for the first time that I might be currently enjoying the best of it.

To give weight to this thought I've been noticing how much busier the path has been over the last few days, with today being no exception. As the morning draws to a close I find myself walking a short stretch with a friendly couple who look and sound as though they've mistakenly wandered out of the original Glastonbury Festival and have been trying to find their way back in for the last 40 years. They've recently walked the Camino de Santiago de Compostela, the world-famous pilgrimage, in Spain. They speak enthusiastically about the communal spirit they encountered on the walk.

They tell me that they often come and spend a long weekend walking this section of the Coast Path because they find that it too has this same sense of comradeship. 'I'm beginning to see that' I say. It's definitely true that I've met and talked to more fellow walkers in the last couple of days than the whole trip combined up to this point. The isolation offered by the Coast Path is of course one of the reasons I'm attempting this challenge. Yet, as the sun shines brightly in the cloudless sky above my sandal-clad comrades and I, it's difficult to think of anywhere else I'd rather be. Over the next 20 minutes or so, until we eventually part company, we continue to chat and swap stories and they even offer to take my tent away for me. They live near Poole and say I'm welcome to swing by and pick it up when I get to the finish line. I politely decline having vowed to myself to use the cumbersome deadweight more often from this point on. As I leave them behind I wonder how many times over the coming weeks I'll curse that decision.

My digs for tonight however are in the tiny but picturesque Port Gaverne. I've elected to stay at the pub here instead of over the hill at the neighbouring Port Isaac due to the inflated prices of the latter. Apparently, Port Isaac playing host to the filming of an ITV drama series called Doc Martin is the reason behind every potential bed for the night being double the expected price... each to their own. I arrive in Port Gaverne in time for a late lunch. My sweaty processed sausage snack and melted Mars Bar hit the spot and are enough for me to work up a healthy thirst. I check into the pub and take residence on a table outside in the sunshine, ale in hand, contentedly gazing out to sea. Two chaps of about my age who I remember passing on the path earlier in the day join me briefly after introducing themselves. They are on a week's walking holiday and are using a carrier service. This means their luggage is taxied from place to place for them and they don't have to carry any packs. I politely explain to them that this is cheating but they're having none of it. They swig down a pint and continue on to Port Isaac where they're staying tonight. Wealthy Doc Martin enthusiasts no doubt.

The next morning I leave Port Gaverne on the steeply climbing road towards Port Isaac. The going is strenuous from the outset as I descend and ascend with muscle-aching familiarity. Scores of seabirds dance above me in the orange glow of the early morning sunshine. The trail clings courageously to the hillside as it undulates in a manner that suggests it's attempting to shake the path off into the waves below.

I arrive at the pretty cottages that make up Port Quin. Also known as 'the village that died' due to a 19th Century tragedy whereby by all the men of the village were drowned at sea during a fishing trip. This lead to the women of the village being forced to abandon their homes, leaving Port Quin to fall into ruin. I stare out at the currently calm, turquoise (I'm definitely using it too many times now) sea as I amble past the tiny village of the damned. So many different things to so many people; a walking companion, a livelihood or an untimely end.

The walking continues to be challenging and breathtakingly beautiful until I arrive at the sandy beaches of Polzeath, where I stop for lunch. A short while thereafter and the path has flattened out and the going is easy as Harry Enfield appears up ahead. I do a comical double take but it's definitely him, walking alongside a small terrier dog. The path is single file and so I stand aside to let him pass.

'Oh, no it should be me letting you pass, you're the one carrying the backpack.'

'No worries at all' I say and we briefly exchange weather-related pleasantries as he walks by. The whole exchange lasts only seconds but is a totally surreal experience. I think largely because I'm out here in the middle of nowhere and am not really prepared for the appearance of TV comedians.

Over the next few minutes I think of all the 'funny' things I could have said to Harry Enfield to make him want to instantly be my friend. I should've opened with '*Only me!*' I decide to text Tasha and tell her about my experience mingling with the stars. After a minute or so she replies with this text, written here word for word exactly as it was sent: 'Did you ask him to use his shower?' I may live to be a hundred and never understand the complex intricacies of this woman's mind.

The walking over the next hour or so is easy going as the path gently winds its way onwards. I inadvertently commit beetle genocide as they suddenly swarm the ground in front of me in Biblical-plague-like quantities. The day is turning into an emotional rollercoaster; first Enfield and now hundreds of gory deaths on my conscience. I'm apologetically wiping the gooey remains of entire families, communities even, from the soles of my boots using a tuft of grass when I hear a voice holler from behind me.

'It would've been better for the image if your bag had been orange rather than green but I got some good shots anyway.' I look up, perplexed, and see a bearded, middle-aged man approaching me with a large camera. 'Hope you don't mind but I've been walking some ways back and have taken some photos with you in them?'

'Oh, er no... No not at all.' He has an American accent and this, combined with his baseball cap and general attire, instantly remind me of John Malkovich's character in the film Empire of the Sun.

'I gotta tell you I didn't think the UK would be this beautiful' he says as he stares ahead at the picturesque view with, my final destination for the day, Padstow visible in the distance.

'Is that Padstow do you know?'

'Yes, I'm pretty sure it is,' I say and we fall in step together and carry on along the path. As we get chatting it transpires that he's actually Canadian not American. He has travelled all the way from Vancouver, where he works as a dentist, just to walk this section of the South West Coast Path. Even though, as he explains, he is an obsessive walker, this still amazes me. To think that this incredible trail is known of and sought after the world over.

I've made a point of not using the real names of anyone I meet along the way up to this point (Harry Enfield notwithstanding) so I'll call this fellow Basie, which is the name of Malkovich's character in the aforementioned Spielberg flick. We continue across sandy beaches and gently winding cliffs until we eventually reach the ferry crossing past Rock Beach that will take us into Padstow. It's the first ferry crossing of the trail and I'm surprised to note a touch of childlike excitement as I haul my giant backpack onto the seat beside me, much to the distain of the other passengers crowded into the small uncomfortable fishing boat.

When we arrive in Padstow we instinctively head for the nearest pub where Basie orders us two pints of Guinness. I'm not a Guinness drinker and fear the worst when he downs his in record time. Over the next few hours we break through the constraints of our social barriers by getting blind steaming drunk on the thick black nectar. As generally happens on these occasions we dutifully bare our souls; I explain the best I can my reasons for this trip: the insomnia and the general longing for a different direction in life. He does likewise with tales of a separation and desire to rediscover some kind of drive or purpose beyond that of plaque removal and root canals.

When I confess that I still, for my sins, enjoy the very occasional cigarette Basie pushes back the baseball cap over his bald scalp, exactly as John Malkovich would do, and proclaims 'I've lost good buddies, Steve. Damn good buddies.' For some reason this causes me to burst out laughing, which could've gone down badly, but thankfully just evokes the same reaction in him and from this point on everything gets a bit chaotic.

I recall being shown some spectacular photographs of trails through the mountains and forests of Canada. Then we're in a taxi and I'm explaining to the patient driver that I've no idea where the campsite I'm staying at is and finding it impossible to comprehend that he wouldn't have this information already. Basie at some point departs for whichever hotel he's staying in and I'm eventually dropped off at the first campsite the driver is able to find. As far as I can fathom I then decide that this is the perfect evening to try out wild camping for the first time. I head back to the coast in the setting sun to root out a picturesque spot.

Saturday Night in Newquay, Hedgehog Ice Cream and Seals!

When I awake, my head feels as though Simon Callow has climbed inside through my ear hole during the night and sat on my brain screaming as loud as he can for six solid hours. I'm lying on my side on the floor of the tent, without a ground mat. The whole right side of my body is one aching mass and my uninflated travel pillow is covered in a layer of drool. I clamber outside into the piercing early morning sunlight. The tent is erected next to a dry-stone wall at the edge of a field adjoining the path itself. I would probably struggle to find a more obvious or less suitable spot along the entire Coast Path. I drink down a whole bottle of water in one long swig and begrudgingly begin to pack up the tent. I'm still fully clothed from yesterday so that at least saves me one task.

I stagger along the path trying to straighten my spine and get some kind of feeling back in my right buttock. I've only been walking a short distance when I come across a giant sinkhole in the hillside. It's the size of a large house. The new Rolly, Rolly 2, on his maiden voyage today, advises me that this is a collapsed cave. I take a minute to thank my lucky stars that I didn't happen upon this hole last night and wake up this morning at the bottom of it.

The going is generally flat and I'm grateful for a refreshing sea breeze that helps to ease the effects of my slowly dissipating hangover. I walk across the sandy beach at Harlyn Bay and on past a striking lifeboat station before reaching the lighthouse at Trevose head where I finally collapse for lunch and a short siesta. I start to feel more human as I make my way onwards towards Constantine Bay.

Some while later a small Jack Russell being chased by a man that looks like a slightly overweight Pee Wee Herman appears on the path ahead of me. I arrest the progress of the mutt by making a fuss of it whilst the out-of-breath owner catches up. He thanks me and tells me the animal has unfortunately worked out how to free itself from a recently purchased lead. He has been chasing it on and off for the entire day. We chat for a while and after commenting that I look like I've been dragged through a hedge backwards he wishes me luck for the rest of the journey.

My energy levels are low and my right leg is causing me some pain, presumably a consequence of my intoxicated bed-making skills. As I hobble onwards I reach a sign advising me I'm now entering Booby's Bay. I take a photo of the sign and send it to some friends over WhatsApp with the caption: 'Alright leave this to me, I'll investigate.' Alas the bay does not quite live up to its name and so I limp onwards towards my resting place for the day: Treyarnon Bay.

My only options for the night are the YHA on the beachfront or a second night under the canvas... and so I obviously make straight for the first youth hostel of the journey. The dorm room is basic but cheap and I'm tired enough to be grateful for anything over and above the tent. I'm sat on the beach later that evening staring up at streaks of bright red and pink sky through the dusk clouds. The black shimmering sea is filled with silently bobbing gulls, allowing the waves to carry them up and down.

After a long while I turn to walk back towards the glowing lights of the hostel when the headlights of a van appear in the distance and rumble up to the main entrance. There is loud singing and chanting coming from within as a second van appears. A rugby team on tour booked into the hostel for the night. Excellent news. The friendly girl at reception advises me that my dorm room won't be invaded as she's ensured they're all housed in the other three rooms. I thank her extensively for this and make my way past the drunken chorus and up the stairs. It's a loud night but after a number of hours my tired bones and weary mind finally give in to a deep dreamless sleep.

As the sun rises over the boisterous turquoise (seriously, stop saying turquoise) waves the next morning I'm already strolling the rocky coastline out of Treyarnon. My leg is still causing me some discomfort so I've been forced to neck back some ibuprofens with my Weetabix. There is a powerful wind this morning that marks a stark contrast to the sunny, summer-like days I've been enjoying recently. The walking is easy for the first stretch leading to the stunning Porthcothan Bay. I'm not the only early bird out and about as surfers fill the sea here, taking advantage of the wind driven waves.

The next stretch through to Watergate Bay is the north Cornish coast at its finest. Far reaching views in both directions as I cling to the cliff edge in the blowing wind. The path winds in and out of rocky coves with steep climbs and descents thrown in all over the shop. As the blustery conditions reach their crescendo I'm almost at 45 degrees just to stay upright. A man with a large grey sergeant major moustache passes me in the opposite direction. The fierce wind is behind him as he comically flails about the place with limbs that seem to have minds of their own. As we pass each other he shouts through a tightly enclosed hood:

'Doesn't get any better, lost my rain cover back there... don't know why we do this to ourselves... Enjoy your day.'

'You too. Best of luck' I shout in return.

I reach the Bedruthan Steps: huge jagged rocks that rise up in a line along the sandy beach. Rolly spins me a yarn about one of them being called the Samaritan because a ship once crashed into it and spilled its cargo of food supplies for the locals to nab. Then on to Watergate Bay and three miles of walking across the sand with the vast rocky cliffs as a foreboding backdrop. The popular surfing resort of Newquay, where I'm due to stay the night, is within view for most of the day. I stop to gaze lovingly at a buzzard in flight. The graceful manoeuvring of the birds of prey along the coastline has already become one of the stand out highlights of the trip so far.

Later that afternoon I'm sprawled out on a bench in the town of Porth, just outside Newquay, taking a breather. An elderly lady approaches me and enquires how far I've walked. A timely ego boost ensues as she praises my resolve and proclaims that she wishes more young people would follow my example of exploration rather than 'Swanning off to Thailand and partaking in lord knows what,' for their gap years. I decide not to mention that I'm nearly forty and really should be at work.

I check into a hotel in Newquay offering rooms for £30 a night. I'm slightly fearful as it happens to be a Saturday night in the stag do capital of the South West. However, I needn't have worried as it becomes immediately apparent that I'm roughly 50 years below the average age of the rest of the hotel guests. There is a bingo hall and a poster advertising a Frank Sinatra tribute act performing later that night in the main dining hall. Saturday night in Newquay sorted!

In truth, after taking a wander around the town and grabbing a bite to eat, I spend the evening in my room listening to Jim Bob reading an audio version of his novel Driving Jarvis Ham. I've been gone 16 days and walked some 190 miles; nearly a third of the journey gone already. I'd expect by now Tasha, along with my family and friends, are all in fits of deep depression, missing me uncontrollably and counting down the minutes until I return. They're probably all on the phone to each other now talking about me. Or maybe having a 'We miss Steve' get-together where they tearfully swap Steve stories as a giant screen displays pictures of my face in the background.

The next morning begins with a walk through the unattractive high streets of the town centre. Peppered with plastic pint glasses, beer cans and half-eaten bags of chips covered in rivers of ketchup and mayonnaise. The occasional puddle of vomit and accompanying stench contaminate the morning sea air. The total silence, save for the feasting gulls, as I sift my way through the debris conjures up post-apocalyptic images from numerous movies. This all changes soon enough however as I move from the midst of a ghost town into the invigorating bustle of the attractive working harbour.

I then finally begin to climb out of Newquay, via a pleasant enough residential area, and on to open country and clifftops in the bright sunshine. A short easy stretch follows to take me to the tidal bridge crossing over the River Gannel. Rolly gives me fair warning that much of today's hike to Perranporth will be across beaches and sand dunes. He also points out, with a touch of arrogance in my opinion, that I've apparently wandered straight past 'Huers Hut', a white brick structure stood overlooking Newquay bay. This isn't the first time something of this nature has happened and I wonder if I'm subconsciously entering into some kind of trance like state whilst walking; probably not advisable whilst traversing the clifftop paths.

It's generally thought (by which I mean I've decided) that as far as the noble art of thinking is concerned walkers fit into two distinct categories. The first is the walker who walks to think. The walk is where you sort all your problems out and return to normal life with an action plan at the ready. The second is the walker who walks to not think. Whereby the walk is the only place where you are able to switch off, clear your head and focus purely on the journey in front of you. Although from time to time I fit into both of these categories I'm predominantly from the latter camp. Walking to me, and in particular the long-distance trail, is life brought back to its purest and simplest form. All that matters is in front of you; just put one foot in front of the other. Walk, eat, walk, find a place to sleep and repeat. It's concerning me however that I may be entering into the spirit of this mind-set a touch too literally and wandering zombie-like around the most beautiful coastline in the world without noticing half of it.

I vow to stop and smell the flowers more often from here on in. A timely conclusion as I enter a particularly picturesque stretch overlooking Crantock Beach heading towards Holywell. An army of seabirds perform an intricate swooping and diving display above me as the sunlight dapples the hillside path. Lower down, hidden within the flowering hedgerows, a choir of invisible songbirds provide the angelic soundtrack. All the while the glistening sea laps seductively at the golden sands far below my dusty boots as they tread cautiously onwards so as to avoid the countless insects on their daily commute. The increasing presence of all manner of creepy crawlies provides confirmation of summer's pending, triumphant arrival. How's that for noticing your surroundings?

As I reach Holywell I spot the elderly lady I met in Porth the day before and we get chatting for a second time. She is the first fellow walker I've met to advise me to keep lugging the tent around. She points out that accommodation will get a good deal punchier once I hit the south coast. I have already made up my mind to hang on to it, to be honest, but it's good to hear from someone who doesn't think I'm a fool to keep hauling the extra weight around. There are days when it still feels like an albatross around my neck but in general I've gotten used to it. We wish each other well and I head off into the sand dunes.

I'm not far into the slog across the dunes before the novelty of clambering up loose sand hills and sliding down the other side has well and truly worn off. My boots are full of sand and the humid heat has left me covered in a clammy sweat. By the time I finally arrive in Perranporth I'm exhausted and emitting an odour that combines pickled onions and wet dog. I'm staying in a room above a pub on the seafront. The place itself isn't one of the most beautiful spots on the path so far and first impressions are of a scaled down Newquay. The pub, with Sky Sports, happy hour and ham, egg and chips for dinner backs up this assertion. I'm not complaining however, as it's cheap, friendly and I quite fancy some ham, egg and chips for dinner. After washing enough times to remove most of the sand from my sun-reddened body and scoffing down the aforementioned English staple, I wander down to the beach and watch the surfers in the evening sun with an ale or two for company.

I can still taste the toothpaste the following morning when the path takes me into a new and alien landscape. The twelve-and-a-half-mile slog from Perranporth to Portreath travels through a long since abandoned mining area. The track winds through jagged exposed rocks revealing scores of hidden caves, mineshafts and the ruins of old tin-mining buildings. The green, blue and turquoise (I could use *azure...* is that the same as turquoise?) landscape of the previous few days is replaced with cold shades of orange and brown. The whole scene reminds me of Tom Baker era Doctor Who and I'm expecting to see a Zygon appear from behind a rock or hear Elisabeth Sladen screaming for me to come and rescue her. (Note to self: this makes you sound like a nerd, remember to replace with something much cooler for the second draft).

Rolly advises me that the caves and mineshafts dotted across the landscape around me are full to bursting point with bats, including some rare species. I transfer into brave explorer mode and fearlessly clamber up to a cave entrance. It's dark. Seriously dark. Picture darkness... yep, this is *much* darker. I creep tentatively inside on tiptoes like I'm in an episode of Scooby Doo. I'm just reaching for my trusty pocket torch when I remember: I don't have a trusty pocket torch. I turn to the trusty old light on my phone instead, which rallies spectacularly and shines a brilliant light, illuminating the one-millimetre area directly surrounding my phone. Oh well, a gallant effort thwarted only by a completely unavoidable lack of resources.

The walking is challenging with plenty of tiring climbs but the views as I reach Cligga Head are worth every drop of perspiration. That being said it's a welcome, if slightly surreal sight, when I happen across a small café nestled between the cliffs at Chapel Porth. I consult Rolly and sure enough he is aware of this isolated haven for the coastal rambler. Furthermore, he insists that I try the 'Hedgehog.' This turns out to be Cornish ice cream smothered in Cornish clotted cream and rolled in honey roasted hazelnuts. When in Rome... As I'm stood at the counter, waiting for my order to be expertly constructed and visibly salivating, I note a sign on the wall proudly proclaiming: 'All our bacon and sausages are fried in Cornish clotted cream.' I briefly entertain the idea of asking the friendly owner taking my order if she'll marry me.

Hedgehog in hand, I sit myself at one of the outside tables looking out to sea. After a short while a small crowd has gathered and the seating area is full. It's as though the café is a lighthouse for walkers. There's a group of folks wearing matching t-shirts with 'The Big 630' written on them. I get talking to them and discover that one amongst their number is walking the whole Coast Path for charity and the others are joining him for certain stretches along the way. I explain sheepishly that I'm not doing this for charity but that, although I don't have an enthusiastic entourage with me at this *exact* moment, my friends did give me their guarantee that they'd come and visit me along the way... so I'm sure this will happen any day now.

When I've dispatched the delicious Hedgehog, I stand looking down at my backpack, wearily contemplating heaving the blasted thing over my shoulders once more. Just then the café owner appears behind me holding a flapjack the size of my foot. She has overheard me saying I'm walking the whole path and sends me on my way with a complimentary example of her cooking prowess. I consider the marriage proposal for a second time. She is maybe twenty years older than me but I figure if everything I'd be eating, post-our-wedding-day, was fried in clotted cream then this probably wouldn't be an issue, as I'd be unlikely to make fifty.

Throughout the afternoon, the mining remains continue to adorn the cavernous coastline. I can see tomorrow's destination of St Ives in the distance as the gulls and guillemots gather in the skies above. I pass several hang gliders somewhere near St Agnes and take a few moments to enviously observe them floating amongst the seabirds in the gentle afternoon breeze.

Just as my feet start to ache I begin the descent into Portreath, where I'm booked into a room above one of the two local pubs. It's currently undergoing renovation so yours truly has negotiated yet another bargain basement price.

Portreath appears to be going through a process of gentrification, becoming a more upmarket holiday getaway, perhaps. There are countless new homes under construction and an almost entirely new town feels as though it's emerging. The pub I'm staying in is evidence of this transformation. It's part way between an old fashioned local pub complete with fruit machine and fluffy carpets and its new, trendy guise with industrial style furniture and selection of craft beers. After a meal of fish and chips, served on a chopping board, I order an ale and I call my folks. I then call Tasha and have a frank discussion regards the continued lack of things fried in clotted cream in our daily lives. A situation, I advise, that we both must strive to remedy.

The next morning at breakfast I'm mulling over the prospect of the day's long 18-mile hike to St Ives; trying to decide if I'm due a second rest day. The odour my clothes are emitting doesn't seem quite as violent as just prior to previous wash day, but I'm conscious that I may have simply become accustomed to that particular stench. I study the face of the pub landlady as she pours my coffee for any signs of veiled disgust. Nothing. Although she does, very kindly, insist on making me a cheese butty to take away with me. So perhaps there's a hidden subtext in there somewhere.

A couple of early tough climbs shortly after leaving Portreath rid me of any further thoughts of relaxation. It's not long however before the walking becomes much easier as the path settles atop the steep cliffs for a prolonged stretch. The warm bright sunshine is the perfect accompaniment to the lush green clifftops and hedgerows bustling with songbirds and buzzing insects. The cloudless blue skies complete the dreamy scene as I wander on contentedly.

After an hour or two I reach the beautiful Godrevy with its impressive lighthouse, perched on its own island amongst the gently purring waves. I stop for an early lunch and sit happily on the cliff edge munching away at my pre-prepared cheese butty. A brief movement from down below on the rocky shoreline catches my eye. I stare downwards for a moment whilst the truth slowly dawns on me. The collection of large rocks strewn over the pebbles below are in fact a group of about twenty seals, basking lazily in the midday sun. At last I'm seeing a glimpse of what Rolly and numerous passers-by have been promising in abundance for days. With a gigantic smile plastered across my wide-eyed face I lie on my belly watching them, with my head poking out over the cliff edge.

I snap hundreds of photographs from this secretive vantage point, like a member of the paparazzi clicking away at some unsuspecting celebrities in their swimming costumes on a beach in Majorca. Instead of a telescopic lens however, I have a cheap smartphone. As a result, I have hundreds of pictures of distant blurry rocks on a nondescript shoreline. I care not though, as I continue to watch the beautiful creatures sunbathing, I feel as though the world is a pretty wonderful place, all things considered.

After dragging myself away I continue along the clifftops for a while longer before arriving at another section of sand dunes. They stretch off into the distance and my feet and leg muscles give a little wince at the prospect. I decide to remove the boots and socks, roll up the trousers and walk along the beach through the gently lapping waves, rather than across the dunes. The scene feels more like the south of France than England in April. The white sands merge seamlessly with the royal blue sea and the horizon in the distance is a perfect straight line. The clear sky above is no more than a single shade of blue lighter. Gulls sit motionless in the water, eyeing me as I pass in the warmth of the afternoon sunlight.

Yet, as feared, it does not take long for the feeling of serenity to be replaced with aches and grumbles as the humid heat becomes stifling and my pace slows on the sand underfoot. By the time I reach the mouth of the estuary, which will take me around the town of Hayle and back down to St Ives, I'm exhausted. Forward another hour or so as I approach Hayle and I'm grizzling like a stroppy child and am just about ready to drop. Rolly is banging on about some historical swing bridge that I simply *must* see, whilst my pack seems now to be physically pushing me to floor.

Under different circumstances I'm sure Hayle is a lovely Cornish town with plenty going for it. At this moment, however, I'm willing it out of existence. I pause outside a giant supermarket that looks like an art gallery and catch my breath. I've walked my daily average already and still have another five or six miles to go before I reach St Ives. I consider changing my plans and finding a bed for the night here in Hayle. I could then have a half day tomorrow instead of a day off and just walk the last few miles in the morning. I go back and forth on this for a few minutes, unsure of what to do. What would Jim Bob do? Probably pen a pun-laced masterpiece perfectly encapsulating the shortcomings of the modern world. Hmmm. I mean I'd like to hear it, but it doesn't seem like a realistic action plan for my current situation.

In the end, I gallantly resolve to carry on. As a result, I'm feeling pretty heroic as I hobble out of Hayle back along the other side of the estuary. Some way along I meet a woman, out on a day's hike, who is also heading to St Ives. She is a clear foot taller than me and resembles a young Annie Lennox, with cropped bleached hair. She is striding at pace with walking poles but, seeing no doubt, that my spirits are dampened she slows her pace to match mine and we walk the final four or so miles together. I go through the (by now mechanical) telling of my journey plans and she reacts with pleasing enthusiasm. She is completing the same journey as myself but one weekend at a time instead of all in one go.

As the path winds its way through affluent residential areas and strips of woodland, we swap stories concerning some locations already passed. She stayed in the same pub as me in Clovelly and passionately loves Verity in Ilfracombe. We chat too about places still ahead of us and then she vocalises something that's been quietly concerning me for a while now. The prospect that by the time I hit Lands' End in a few days the very best of this trail will already be behind me. Sobering stuff.

Eventually we arrive in St Ives with the afternoon sunshine still in full swing. We stop for an ice cream at the first seaside café we reach before wishing each other well and saying our goodbyes. I book into another hotel catering for the more senior clientele. As with the hotel in Newquay, it's wondrously inexpensive and boasts its own bingo lounge. I mean what more could you want? The lady at reception is clearly slightly perplexed by my presence but greets me with a smile. I book a room for two nights having decided a day off enjoying the sights of St Ives, is definitely in order.

The following morning, once the Weetabix are duly dispatched, I head off to find a launderette and some entertainment for the day. St Ives is a beautiful place with narrow cobbled streets adorned with art galleries, museums and independent retailers. There is a hive of trendy eateries surrounding the picture postcard harbour and, although the weather is distinctly greyer than yesterday, the whole town bustles with activity. Whilst waiting for the old pants and socks to go through their, somewhat-less-than-weekly service, I wander around a fishing museum and grab lunch at a swanky pasta restaurant. I think one of the two ladies on the table next to mine used to present Blue Peter... but I can't be sure.

A pleasant afternoon is spent exploring the town and lounging by the harbour listening to an audiobook of PG Wodehouse stories. All in all, my second day off is a vast improvement on the first. That being said, as I lie waiting for sleep's embrace later that night, I'm nonetheless desperate to get back on the trail.

Slush Puppies at the End of the World, Open Air Rehearsals and the Paris Hotel

The walk to Zennor the next morning is a short but challenging one. At only six and a half miles, it's much shorter than any day's walk up to this point. In part this is because I've bookmarked Zennor as a place I want to visit. It's famous for its connection to D.H. Lawrence, who once described it as the most beautiful place in the world. It's also home to the Tinners Arms, apparently a contender for the best pub on the whole Coast Path. Fair enough. I wasn't able to book a room at the Tinners but have secured lodgings at a nearby B&B.

The walk begins easily enough with a stroll out of St Ives, past the Tate Gallery, on to an area called Clodgy Point. The weather is threatening to turn and the waves below me are becoming agitated. The going then gets very tough, very quickly. The landscape becomes rugged and the path increasingly treacherous as it winds in and out and sometimes over jagged rock formations. The ground is slippery and during the steeper climbs I have to cling on to the rocks to stay upright. Although the descents and ascents are not as vast as in some of the earlier sections, they are more acute than anything I've yet experienced. At times, it feels more like rock climbing than walking.

As you might expect the views are simply stunning and there is a real sense of remoteness here that I've not felt since the opening few days in North Devon. I then pass a strange, far-too-modern-looking uniform, stone circle with a path of stepping stones leading to it. I observe a few nearby signposts and consult Rolly to discover that the circle belongs to a campsite not far from here. It makes up part of a short circular walk they've constructed for the enjoyment of their clientele. As I walk across a meticulously laid out boardwalk section, I'm sure I detect a hint of scorn in Rolly's usually deadpan delivery.

Shortly after this I stop for lunch in a small clearing, sheltered from the strengthening winds. Whilst I gorge on my faux salami and accompanying Mars Bar, I see a young rabbit emerge tentatively from underneath a large rock. It hops around excitedly for a minute or so before settling and chomping contentedly on the grassy verge a few metres away from me. I wonder how our Bovril is getting on and picture him sprawled out under the dining table or perhaps ripping to shreds any personal items that anyone has been foolish enough to leave lying around; his most favourite of all leisure activities.

It's early afternoon when I arrive in the pretty village of Zennor. Before checking into my B&B I wander around the ancient parish church and immediate surrounding countryside which, with good reason, has been designated an Area of Outstanding Natural Beauty. After what I deem to be a respectable length of time soaking up the atmosphere I head for the pub. The Tinners Arms is an attractive old-fashioned pub where everything seems to be made of wood. I plonk myself on one of the stools, all of which are made from emptied beer barrels, at a small table and make myself comfortable. I sample their eponymous ale and am duly impressed.

I chat for some time to the friendly landlady and barman about everything from correct tyre pressures to pre-War Scandinavian politicians. As I'm advising them that I've never actually read Women in Love; into the pub arrives the chap walking the Coast Path for charity, from a few days ago, complete with entourage and 'The Big 630' t-shirts. Inevitably, as the ale flows freely, we all end up pushing our empty barrels together and chatting the evening away. Discussing everything from early Eighties synth-pop to the downfall of MFI. I don't recall the journey back to my B&B with complete clarity, dear reader, but I feel confident it will have been conducted with a quiet and subtle dignity.

As I set off along the footpath leading out of Zennor, to rejoin the Coast Path early the next morning, the rain is falling hard. The skies are a thunderous dark grey and the winds are relentless. The twelve-mile trip to St Just is promising to be a tough one. The path picks up where it left off the previous afternoon with a steep slippery descent down a rocky hillside to a bridge crossing a small stream. To compound matters further I've picked up a bit of a head cold, which is definitely slowing me down as I climb back out of the valley under sheets of driving rain.

The path continues undulating through the rocky landscape for a brief spell before I'm clambering down into another valley. It continues like this for some time with the increasingly poor conditions robbing me of any views and ensuring my pace is slow and cumbersome. Even the gulls are absent as I inch along the single-track path with a sheer drop to the raging sea beside me. It would be an ideal moment to bolster the brave explorer motif, but I'm too busy feeling sorry for myself. I continue past Bosigran Head and again climb down, this time into Porthmoina Cove.

It's around here, as I'm mulling over the number of place names in Cornwall that start with either Porth or Trey, that the ghostly remains of mining buildings start to materialise through the mist and rain. Giant tumbling chimneys and half-standing stone structures that take on an eerie feel silhouetted against the stormy backdrop. As I pass through these remnants of

Cornwall's once-thriving industry, the path is constantly splintering off in several directions, with the poor visibility making it increasingly difficult to navigate.

Just past the lighthouse at Pendeen which, to be frank, I can't really see through the rain, I arrive at Geevor Mine. The landscape becomes even more industrial as the building remains are joined by huge slag heaps dotted either side of the path. I then come to Levant Mine, which is owned by the National Trust and has been lovingly restored and opened up to the public. This adds a surreal edge to the day as through the murky and blustery conditions families of tourists emerge from a pay and display car park. I pass a gift shop and an ice cream van before rounding a corner and being instantly transported back to the remote and stormy isolation of a few minutes prior. I briefly wonder if I've hallucinated the last hundred yards.

By the time I reach the third and final mine at Botalleck I'm very nearly spent. The rain has not eased up for a second and the wind is actually continuing to strengthen. The path again splits like a maze and the waymarkers disappear. At some point I take a wrong turning. I spend an hour or so finding my way back to the Coast Path. Soon after this I arrive at a golf course. If I was in a pram and had some toys with me, I would throw those toys out of the pram. If I had a pair of knickers I would twist them, that is to say I would get them in a twist... the knickers.

Sometime later I arrive at Cape Cornwall which, even in these conditions, is arrestingly beautiful. I stop and stare out past the lighthouse to the still raging sea. The rain at last eases slightly and the distant cries of seabirds are audible for the first time today. I take my pack off and collapse like a drowned rat onto the muddy ground. I spend a few minutes here, transfixed. This gives me the strength to face the final mile or so trek inland to the town of St Just, where I'm booked into a pub for the evening. I leave the Coast Path and trudge along first a farm track and then a B-road, until I eventually reach the town's attractive central market square, with its imposing clock tower.

After the longest bath in the history of intelligent life I make my way, shrivelled like a prune, down to the pub for dinner. Conscious that most evening meals up to now have consisted, either in part or in total, of chips, I decide to splash out on the house speciality. I'm presented with a monkfish curry. Now, I don't know to what extent the trauma of the day behind me is a factor here; but I have to tell you, dear reader, that the Commercial Inn in the town of St Just, Cornwall, Great Britain, serves the best monkfish curry in the entire world. Later that evening I call several loved ones to share this important discovery but, if anything, I'm met with little more than widespread apathy.

I head off early the next morning, brimming with excitement at the prospect of reaching Lands' End. Even though Lands' End isn't technically half distance, it's very much the psychological halfway point of the trail. The major turning point, from which you begin the long journey home. I'm still fighting off a bit of a cold but have dramatically improved since yesterday in that regard. As has the weather, which has gone from one extreme to the other. As I rejoin the path just the other side of Cape Cornwall, the sun is illuminating the clear blue skies and the sea is a calm, shimmering blanket. The gulls and songbirds have emerged from their hiding places and now fill the sky, both physically and audibly.

The going is relatively flat and easy as I push, on overlooking splendid rocky and sandy beaches. The sun is beating down and I'm conscious of not applying adequate quantities of the trusted factor 30 before setting off this morning. I can feel the beginnings of the burn on my face. I squint up at the sky and see the silhouette of a kestrel flying alongside me just over the hillside. It glides mesmerizingly, rising and falling as I smile up at it adoringly. I imagine it following me round the entire trail to Poole Harbour and dream up a lengthy canon of exciting adventures for the two us. Incredible, life-affirming stories, which reveal the unbreakable bond between a handsome wanderer and his wild hunter bird. Tamed only by its unwavering respect and loyalty towards this mysterious man of nature. I would stand atop the cliffs calling to it (I could speak Kestrel obviously.) The camera would pan out as the bird swoops down from nowhere and perches on my shoulder. I will name it *KestWing* (that needs work).

When I reach Lands' End a few hours later the day is still a fine and clear one, although a stiff breeze now chills the bones. It's difficult to know where to start when attempting to describe Lands' End. The isolation and tranquillity of the Cornish coastline are replaced with a sort of mini fun fair and hotel complex that might be better suited to Bognor seafront. What the place lacks in beauty it more than compensates for in weirdness. So effectively has this picturesque and significant patch of Cornwall been transformed into a bizarre neon wonderland that it almost defies parody.

The smell of frying burgers, cigarette smoke and sticky candy floss fill the air as I wander through the end of the world. I pass limp rotating hot dogs and people in their pyjamas. Past screaming parents and their defiant spawn, past dilapidated kiosks and... Hang on... SLUSH PUPPIES! Best. Day. Ever. What a truly wonderful and magical place this is.

I order an extra-large raspberry slush and excitedly carry the glowing bright blue cup of goodness through the crowds and out towards a small café by the cliff edge. The café has a sign that reads 'The First and Last Refreshments House in England.' I sling off the pack and sit on a bench in front of the sign to consume my ample beverage. I give myself a few minutes to reflect on the adventure so far and everything that's still to come.

Once the ego is suitably massaged, the aching feet suitably rested and the belly suitably bloated with a pint of blue slush, I don the pack and carry on. After a few yards, I spy the famous Lands' End sign that every visitor is obliged to get a photograph of themselves standing in front of. It displays distances to John O'Groats, New York and the Isles of Scilly. As I approach it however it becomes clear that the aforementioned souvenir snap won't be quite so simple. There is a long queue of people and a sandwich board that advises me it will cost me £18 to have my photograph taken in front of the sign. That's eighteen pounds, for one photograph of me, standing in front of a sign. For this paltry sum, you do of course also get a fourth distance marker added to the sign displaying a destination of your choice. This is of no interest to yours truly and so I sidle up to the small waist height fence that encircles the famous landmark, turn my back to it, smile my best smile and take a picture with my phone. For free.

As I continue on my way I give a pitying look to the chumps still standing in the queue and take a gander at my photograph. What I see smiling back at me alarms me. A bright red sunburnt face, save for the brilliant white of the crow's feet around my eyes, and bright blue lips. Oh, and a blurry sign in the background telling me how far it is to West Bromwich from here. Underneath the sign stands a rotund, angry looking man holding a camera. I use the public facilities to wash the blue from my mouth and plaster on the factor 30. I then sneak back and take another picture, with marginally better results.

I pick up the path again and leave Lands' End behind me. On my way, I pass a small petting zoo as a couple of grubby pre-schoolers with trainers fitted with glowing LED lights throw crisps at some thoroughly miserable looking goats. As the path begins to get more interesting, the people start to

61

disappear and the distant hue and cry of the crowd fades away. Looking back, I see the impressive Armed Knight Rock, sticking out into the sea with a giant hole through its centre.

The walking remains easy as I stick to a hilltop path near the cliff edge. The rocky beaches of Zawn Trevilley and then Mill Bay pass by in the hot afternoon sunshine. Silky waves lap on the sandy shoreline below as noisy gulls glide and swoop across the clear skies above. I'm soon descending into the quintessential Cornish village of Porthgwarra, where I take a moment to rest the feet, by sprawling out on the sand. It turns out that a tasty extra-large Slush Puppy is not a sensible midday beverage when embarking on a twelve-mile hike. Who knew? I'm still belching freely as I clamber to my feet ten minutes later and lumber on.

Later that afternoon, after passing the secluded Porth Chapel beach, I am nearing the end of the days walk. The path leads me into a car park belonging to the Minack Theatre in Porthcurno. Not being the most cultured of fellows my knowledge of the Minack is limited. I have though, been lead to believe that it's a sight to behold. It's therefore with some enthusiasm that I make my sweaty way to the theatre entrance. After paying my ticket fee and convincing the rosy-cheeked lady at reception that she really does want to look after my bag whilst I wander round, regardless of standard procedure, I turn the corner and see the theatre in front of me. Blimey.

The open-air theatre is carved into the rock face and juts triumphantly out from the cliff edge. I'm dumbstruck at its splendour, feeling as though I've wandered into ancient Rome by mistake. A sensation supported by the Mediterranean-like blue sea, providing a sparkling backdrop in the still warm sunlight. I expect to see a couple of gladiators appear and fight it out to the death at any moment. It occurs to me that in the space of just a few hours I've seen the very worst and very best examples of humankind's effects on this exhilarating coastline.

The tacky entertainment complexes of Lands' End seem of a different world to the architectural triumph that now caresses my optic senses. Caresses my optic senses? What on earth? I'm trying to be theatrical.

The theatre is the brain child of the late Rowena Cade, who started building it in the late 1920s, and never really stopped. There is a fascinating museum onsite that details the history of this ever-evolving masterpiece. I'm also lucky enough to be here as a rehearsal is taking place and so get to experience something of what it would be like to watch a performance here. I can only imagine how wonderful it must be in the evening light with a full crowd. I sit contentedly for a good thirty minutes before making my way to the café, where I sit contentedly for a further thirty minutes. I vow to return here one day to watch a full production.

In the end I begrudgingly tear myself away from the Minack and head for the B&B I'm booked into for the night. During the trip thus far I've more often than not plumped for a room above a pub ahead of a B&B. Tonight's lodgings adequately sum up the reasons behind this decision. Don't get me wrong, the house is perfectly lovely and its owner perfectly pleasant, a tip-top chap in fact. But when all is said and done I'm sleeping in a stranger's spare room. For some, more socially accomplished members of the rambling jet set, this is all part of the charm of long distance walking. Who wants to be in a smelly, impersonal room above a pub when you could be relaxing with new friends in the comfort of their living room? Sharing life stories over a home-cooked meal before retiring to your snug bedroom where, later that night, your new best friend will bludgeon you to death with the delightful art deco style doorstop you were waxing lyrical about over your home-cooked lentil moussaka?

Breakfast the next morning is a communal affair. Myself and the two other guests staying in the house (a young couple looking every bit as uncomfortable as I feel) are positioned around a circular dining table in the kitchen, along with our earnest host. Apart from a brief encounter with the owner the previous evening this is the first time I've met any of my dining companions. I spent the night in the local pub nursing an ale or two before creeping back to my room in the dead of night. Luckily, being a 21st century office worker, I have endured many years of awkward, joyless 'getting to know you' sessions and 'team building' days and so am fully equipped to deal with this situation. I'm able to recite any number of inane questions from a large memorised supply.

Once we've rolled through the full set of introductory platitudes and are tucking into our full English we begin to relax. The couple are on a holiday with no plan. That is to say they have literally got in the car and headed to Cornwall with no idea where they would stay or what they would do. I exclaim my delight at this, as does our increasingly jovial host. 'Do you do that a lot?' I enquire. 'First time, we've only been together a couple of months so this our first holiday.' I reflect on how the impulsiveness of love's young dream can, on occasion, lead you to be sat in someone else's kitchen at 7.30 in the morning with only a sunburnt rambler and a moussaka-making, doorstop wielding murderer for company.

I march off towards the sea to pick up the path a short while later, full of joie de vivre and fried stuff. A steady climb takes me out of Porthcurno, up above the sandy beaches, to reveal the path ahead of me. It's another glorious spring day as I pass the impressively scaly Logan Rock. Rolly advises me that a pair of cohabiting giants are thought to live here, but they must be out enjoying the sunshine, as the rock stands deserted amongst the motionless surface of the water. A series of steep descents and ascents follow, as the path climbs to hilltops with beautiful panoramic views and then drops just as suddenly down into unspoiled coves, with rows of empty wooden fishing boats.

I enter a luscious green woodland section as my ears ring with the sound of hundreds of merrily chirping birds, nestled in the trees all around me. A few yards in, my progress is halted as a young fox wanders on to the path about 30 feet ahead of me. I stand, statuesque, and observe as it sits and cleans its paws, completely unaware of my presence. I silently and, somewhat stealthily, manoeuvre my phone from my pocket. I switch it to camera and very slowly position it to face the still-oblivious creature. My finger is over the button as the fox glances up, sees me and scarpers into the bushes. I get a photo of a woodland track with a small orange blur in one corner. I'm experiencing so many scenes like this; private glimpses of all manner of wildlife that I would not otherwise get to observe. From leaping deer to fearless squirrels that fly, kamikaze, from branch to branch. Whether it be a buzzard taking a nap in the long grass of a farmland field, or a baby rabbit tentatively exploring its new surroundings. Unique moments which all serve to further enrich this incredible trail.

I emerge from the trees into a stunningly beautiful cove. Rolly is unable to confirm with any certainty whether it's St Loy's or Paynter's Cove. He really needs to buck his ideas up. I cross the pebbly beach and weave through a small spattering of two or three houses. The spot is so secluded and has an almost tropical feel to it, contrasted against the rocky cliffs and still calm ocean. I decide that once I've replaced Bill Bryson as the world's premier travel writer and made my inevitable millions, I will live here. I'll probably just buy all the houses so I can have a spare or two for guests.

The sharp climbs and precarious descents continue as the day wears on. It doesn't take long before they start to take their toll and I'm exhausted. My pack is weighing heavy and my feet are throbbing. It's the downhill sections that are causing me the most issues. The concentration required to balance the weight of the pack whilst gingerly descending through jagged rocks, on slippery muddy paths along a cliff edge where tripping isn't an option, is increasingly difficult to maintain. After a while I'm given some respite however as the path levels out in the approach to Kemyel Point. Another rise follows towards Point Spaniard, which takes its name from the Anglo-Spanish War, when a fleet of Spanish ships landed here and subsequently laid carnage to the nearby Penzance.

The since rebuilt Penzance is where my day's walk ends. But first I must negotiate Newlyn and the excellently named Mousehole. Both of which turn out to be unwelcome urban sprawls. To be clear, as I'm aware that anyone who's visited either of these spots and is reading this, is no doubt wondering what on Earth I'm talking about, both spots are, in the grand scheme of things quaint and picturesque Cornish villages or towns. But when you spend all day in the comparative wilderness, marvelling at the wonders of nature, any sudden accumulation of concrete, car engines and retail outlets is sure to be an unwelcome sight. I feel certain that if I was to revisit any one of the coastal settlements that I've callously dismissed, albeit with unsurpassed wit and sophistication, I would find them a welcome and peaceful retreat from city life. It's all context. The context here being that my feet hurt, my pack is slowly but surely remoulding my spine and I'm sweaty and clammy in a way that is as unpleasant as it is unhygienic.

Maintaining the generous spirit of the previous paragraph I'll put my initial opinion of Penzance down to context. Likewise, the pub that I've booked a suspiciously cheap room above. I mean I enjoy the comfort of the tracksuit bottom as much as the next man but, statistically speaking, what are the chances of this being the chosen attire of an entire pub full of patrons? Perhaps there's a leisurewear convention in town that I'm unaware of. My room is dark, stained and (most alarmingly of all) hairy. The latter to such a degree that I decide that, when the time comes, I'll unravel the old sleeping bag rather than peel back the suspect sheets. At least that way I know the source of the stains and hairs on which I lay. That evening I dine on an all-you-can-eat Chinese buffet and spend a pleasant couple of hours talking to friends and family on the phone.

The 14-mile hike to Porthleven the following day begins bright and early, with a stroll along the promenade out of Penzance. The walkway is the only thing separating the railway track on one side from the boisterous sea on the other, which makes for a bracing start to the walk. I'm soon passing St Michaels Mount; an elaborate castle on its own tiny island, accessible only at low tide. A short jaunt through the town of Marazion follows but is mercifully short, if somewhat confusing. Just as I'm starting to think I might be lost I find my way back to the beach and eventually a path leading back up onto the Cornish cliffs.

The going is generally easy along the next stretch but is not lacking in dramatic views, as the sea below begins to work up a temper. There is an inland diversion, due to cliff erosion, to negotiate for a few miles. This takes me along a country lane past a quintessentially English village and over some open farmland, before returning me to the coast. The landscape stretching out in front of and behind me is a contrast of blooming flowers, sandy beaches, jagged rocks and now raging waves. The wind is strong and the looming clouds above threaten to erupt at any moment. Countless gliding gulls and crows are silhouetted against the horizon to complete the richness of the scene. I'm again conscious that there is nowhere on Earth that I would rather be right now.

I walk across the large sandy beach at Perranuthnoe and onwards to Piskies Cove, a baffling oasis of calm tranquil blue waters, before then reaching the astonishing Prussia Cove. A truly beautiful landscape with a rich history of smuggling and shipwrecks. The path here winds through isolated homes perched on the cliff edge, then past an eerie collection of ghostly dilapidated fisherman's cottages left to ruin. The walking continues to be relatively untaxing as I pass Kennegy Sands, round Hoe Point and arrive at Praa Sands. A vast sprawling sandy beach full of revelling surfers. There is a beachside bar and restaurant that tantalisingly tempts me, as I plonk myself unceremoniously down on the sand to consume my lunch rations.

My food supplies have again reached a sorrowful state of affairs. My remaining three Mars Bars have melted down and then been reborn as new, deformed and unappetising shapes. My processed spicy sausage snacks are, well, still processed spicy sausage snacks. Those glorious early lunches of swanky French salamis and handy bite-sized cheeses seem but a distant dream. As I sit munching, the rain begins to drizzle down and forces me to cut short my lamenting. I trudge cumbersomely through the loose sand underfoot for what seems like an age before finally rejoining the path proper. I walk through a scrub land area called Lesceave, which brings with it the re-emergence of reminders of Cornwall's rich mining history. Piles of slag and the ruins of great chimneys once more appear around me.

Frustratingly, the path takes me slightly inland again over the next section, avoiding more coastal erosion no doubt. I can see more ruined mining buildings, practically hanging from the dramatic rocky cliff edges, above the crashing waves. I want to be closer to the cliff edge and begrudge this safety-based diversion decision. Eventually, as Porthleven comes into view, the path at last returns to the coastline. The threatening downpour never emerged and the clouds have now given way to clear blue skies. The wind still packs a punch and the waves below still crash atmospherically, but the scene is more sedate as I continue on my way. As if to verify this assertion, scores of busy rabbits have appeared from nowhere and are grazing merrily in the fields to my left. I spy a grass snake on the path in front of me and stop still to watch as it slithers by.

On the way into Porthleven two unaccompanied dogs appear over the hillside. A black Labrador and a small terrier of some description run towards me, give me a ruddy good sniff and then continue on about their business. Which seems to primarily consist of pawing and barking at rabbit holes. I look about for the owners but none appear. I wait around for five minutes to put my mind at rest, but still nobody arrives. The pair are excitedly running about the place without a care in the world, paying me no attention whatsoever. Yet they are at times precariously close to the cliff edge and I decide that I can't, in all good conscience, just walk away.

I take off my pack and walk over to them to see if they have collars on, but neither do. I glance at my phone and see I have no reception. I try to get them to follow me by offering them a spicy sausage snack. They decline, which must surely say something regards my current luncheon menu. I walk inland, onto the nearest road and continue along it for some time, before I come across a man washing his car outside a red-brick bungalow.

'Excuse me, sorry to trouble you,' I say. 'I'm a little worried as there's a couple of dogs back down the road that I think might be strays. Would you be able to help me at all?'

He looks me up and down and smiles 'A black Lab and a Yorkie?'

'Um, yes. That's them.'

'They belong to the house up the hill,' he says, pointing off at nothing. 'They spend their lives there, nothing to worry about.' I mean it's not much of a story, dear reader, but it was a rollercoaster of emotions at the time, I assure you.

Porthleven is an attractive harbour town with an imposing clock tower that sticks defiantly out to sea. It's reminiscent of

Padstow with its trendy upmarket restaurants and pubs. It appeals to me more than the former though, for reasons I'm not sure of. Possibly it's not quite as overdeveloped and perhaps something in its layout is more attractive. I'm staying in a friendly guesthouse at the top of one of the sides of the valley that the town sits in. From outside I can look down over the small bustling town centre and out to sea. This is a particularly pretty sight after sunset when the entire town is illuminated by hundreds of hanging multi-coloured lights.

I spend that evening in a very pleasant pub near the seafront. I plump for an ale aptly titled Porthleven, courtesy of a local brewery based in nearby Truro. It's a contender for the best of the trip so far. After one or two I get chatting to a chap at the bar. He's possibly in his sixties, has bushy grey sideburns and is wearing a slightly shabby green sweatshirt, that is a smidge on the small side for his generous frame. He is Porthleven born and bred and weaves an engrossing tale, charting the history of the place and how much it's changed in his lifetime. Among many points of interest, he tells me that the impressive clock tower is currently a snooker club venue. I find this somewhat depressing, but he points out that it's better than it sitting empty.

Eventually we get chatting about my journey and he clearly struggles to understand my reasons for attempting it.

'So, you're telling me that you're walking all of the Cornwall Coast Path... on your own?'

'No, I'm walking all of the South West Coast Path on my own... Minehead round to Poole Harbour.'

He looks at me as though he's trying to decide whether or not I'm pulling his leg. He takes another swig of beer before asking, 'Why?'

'It's just something I've wanted to do for a long time, y'know... for fun.'

He takes this in. 'Cause it's this you gotta be weary of son.' He taps his temple with his fore finger. 'All that time with only your own thoughts for company, it's a long old road'. I sense we're in danger of getting a bit philosophical and steer the conversation in a different direction. We discuss the best ales I've tried along the way and he's delighted that the one we're both currently enjoying rates so highly in my estimation. At the end of the evening we say our goodbyes and he wishes me luck for the rest of the trip;

'Well I won't pretend I don't think you're as nuts as a bag of nuts,' (he actually said that), 'But I say good on you.'

Later that night I'm struggling to fall asleep and my mind eventually wanders back to his words. 'All that time with only your own thoughts for company.' What if he's right? What if this trip drives me crazy? What if I can't integrate back into normal society? What if I've spent the last 25 days talking to my guidebook? What if there is no grey side-burned man sitting at the bar? What if I go back there tomorrow and ask after him and am told 'you must mean old Jacob... but he been dead these past thirty years.' What if I am as nuts as a bag of nuts?

Early the next morning I'm climbing out of Porthleven at the beginning of the day's 14-mile slog to the Lizard. The most south-westerly point of mainland Britain. The wind is ferocious and the sky filled with hundreds of noisy gulls. Early on I spy two of them squabbling with a kestrel or a peregrine; I'm never sure which at a distance. The scene is like watching a First World War dogfight, as the three skilled flyers weave and dive at each other, before the gulls are inevitably victorious and chase the other away. Despite the blustery conditions the sun is warm and bright, as the sky and ocean compete over which is the more vivid tone of blue.

After an easy flat section along the hilltops I reach the Loe Bar. The area is designated one of outstanding natural beauty and it's not difficult to see why. The Bar itself is a giant sand bank created by raging storms in the 12th Century. As it formed it cut off the estuary behind it from the sea. This created Loe Pool, the largest freshwater lake in the county. Beautiful it may be but it's not pleasant walking after a while. A long stretch of loose sand that soon becomes a real slog in the strong winds. Thankfully, I eventually climb back up to the clifftop where the path remains flat and unusually straight until I reach a cove called Gunwalloe, a few miles later.

The path becomes a touch more challenging from then on in but is still a good deal less eventful than the average day's walking on this trail. I'm not complaining however as the wind has died down and the summer scenery is a joy to stroll through. The pretty but overpopulated Church Cove follows, before I reach a striking monument on the way to Mullion. It's titled the Marconi Monument and marks the spot where Guillermo Marconi sent the first transatlantic radio signal in 1901. The crowds enjoying Church Cove and visiting the Monument continue, as I arrive at the day's halfway point of Mullion Cove.

I stop for lunch and a milkshake, which I purchased earlier from a small beach café. As I'm sitting, supping contentedly, an elderly gent slips on the serpentine rocks in front of me. He lands head first and splits his nose open with gory results. I rush over to him but his wife and several other passers-by already surround him. After recovering from the shock and resting a while he seems OK, but it won't look pretty for a good while. This area has an abundance of serpentine, which is a startlingly pretty rock, but a very slippery one. I do genuinely therefore question the sense of having stiles made from the material, throughout this section of the Coast Path. The things are deadly and on many occasions I've nearly gone arse about face.

The next few miles take me through an area called Predannack Downs. A landscape that feels totally different to any I've walked through recently. Large open grassy rolling expanses, staying at a consistent level as far as the eye can see. This featureless landscape provides me with an excellent opportunity to work on my album of walking-themed classics. I've been composing this masterpiece, mentally, for a week or so now. The premise is simple enough: take a well-known song from the popular music world and change a word or two so that it sounds like it's about walking. I'll give you an example. You know the PJ & Duncan classic 'Let's get ready to rumble'? Of course you do, well I've changed it to 'Let's get ready ramble.' Sing it to yourself... It's good eh? More recently I've come up with 'Keep strollin' strollin' strollin' strollin'', you know, like that song that says 'Keep rollin' rollin' rollin' rollin'' by Linford Biscuits or whatever he's called. It's a sure-fire money-spinner in the unlikely event that this book doesn't make me my billions. It's always sensible in life to have a robust backup plan.

The path continues in a similar vein until I eventually reach the beautiful chaos that is Kynance Cove. A striking, if ramshackle, collection of jagged cliffs, rocky islands, caves and suchlike. Rolly advises me that one of these islands is named Asparagus Island, but I'm hanged if I can tell you which one. It's impossible not to pause for thought here and watch as the sea crashes in amongst this maze-like jumble. I push on past a small collection of cottages and out towards Lizard Point.

My final destination is a campsite a few miles inland, as I feel it's time the canvas got another outing. The remainder of the walk continues to be relatively flat and when I reach the campsite, I'm astonished at my lack of tiredness. I set up camp and head off to Lizard village to find a chippy. The village has an oddly sparse feel to it as the buildings are situated at great distances from each other, which gives the whole place a remote, Father Ted feel. After sitting in the evening light, eating a bag of chips and looking out at the sea for a while, I make my way back to the tent. It's a surprisingly welcome sight. This is a great spot for camping and I'm feeling as though I might be discovering the outdoors man in me at last.

Stupid tent; I mean what's the point? It's the following morning and I've had three hours and twenty-seven minutes of sleep. Most of which were spent dreaming of erecting an impossible giant tent. Assembling endless poles and hooks and never achieving anything resembling a usable structure. Now here I am; aching, hungry and distinctly dishevelled. Trying in vain to pack the blasted thing back into the appropriate bags - which have all, definitely and without any question, shrunk during the night. 'Well this is it Mr Tent, our sham of a relationship is over. I'll carry you around but from now on you are deadweight to me.' I have plenty more to say to Mr Tent but stop myself, deciding that maintaining a relationship with one inanimate object is probably enough.

After achieving the impossible and reassembling the kit, I'm on my way again and the going is initially easy. The lush green hillsides, dotted with blooming flowers in the morning sunlight, and a chorus of cheery birdsong, all serve to brighten my mood considerably. I'm not far into the trek however when the drops and climbs begin. I pause for breath at the conclusion of the third or fourth steep ascent and consult Rolly regards the day ahead. He advises that this stretch is brimming with basking sharks and I should be able to catch sight of one before long. This is exciting news and there's a spring in the step as I continue on my way.

The walk continues to be challenging over the next few miles. The task is made all the more difficult by the continued abundance of attractive but slippery serpentine stiles. By the time I reach Cadgwith I'm exhausted and decide that an early lunch is in order. I sit watching the numerous boats of varying sizes and descriptions perched on the gently rocking sea. With a start, I realise I have company in the form of a deceased frog sitting centimetres in front of me, gazing lifelessly at my half consumed chocolatey rations. This is the third such departed amphibian I've observed in the last 24 hours. I hope this isn't the beginnings of a biblical plague or deadly killer virus that wipes out all life on Earth. First the frogs started dying, then the budgerigars... That sort of thing.

As I leave Cadgwith a light rain shower awakens the gulls' interest and the birdsong of earlier is replaced by a sustained period of squawks and cries from these characterful sea birds. I pass large numbers of wild ponies over the next few miles, all contentedly munching on the plentiful flora. One decidedly rotund Shetland follows me along the path for a while, sniffing at my backpack before eventually deciding that nothing of interest lay within. The walk has flattened out since lunch and, despite the intermittent showers, the ambiance is that of a serene summertime stroll.

I arrive at the Devil's Frying Pan. A once majestic cave whose roof has at some point collapsed, creating an even more impressive arch surrounding a gigantic hole. Even in the relative calm the sea water froths angrily around, as it's temporarily cut off from the ocean. I can only imagine how incredible this spot must be on a fiercely stormy day. I stay staring, utterly transfixed by the scene. I have already passed a Devil's Mouth at some point recently and am wondering how many other Satanic-themed coastal spots I may have missed along the way. It's evidence of the fear generated by the power and potential devastation of the mighty sea. The most beautiful thing on this planet is also a merciless killer.

A short while later I reach a steep climb that takes me to Beagles Point. Here I'm met with a truly spectacular view of the path ahead of me, including my destination for the day:

Coverack. In light of the latest unpleasant night under the canvas I have booked a room above a pub that sits just off the path itself. The enticingly named Paris Hotel, which sounds like the perfect antidote to the camping experience. Indeed (whilst admittedly not being quite as grand as the name suggests) the pub does not disappoint. A friendly welcoming spot and a decent room with a perfect view of the ocean.

That evening I'm lying in bed watching a constant stream of gulls gliding past my window. It strikes me just how much of this journey so far, I've spent looking up. I've come to understand that there is always a drama being played out above our heads. Most of the time we don't think to look upwards but we should do. There is a whole other world unfolding just outside of our view. Those gulls are *always* up to something.

3. South Cornwall

Ferry Crossings, We Need to Talk About Rolly and Stranded in Plymouth

The next day, for reasons I'm unsure of, I've set myself the mammoth task of a 23-mile hike to Falmouth, including a ferry crossing over the Helford Estuary. So, it's unfathomably early in the morning when I set off from Coverack. Leaving the Paris Hotel behind me and accompanied by a noisy army of gulls, I march purposefully onwards in the bright light of the crisp new day. The gulls swoop around me as if investigating what on earth I'm doing here at this time of the morning. Rolly advises me that much of the going today will be sedate and easy, so I exude something of a ruddy-faced confidence as I make my way onwards.

Indeed, as if to confirm this, the day begins without the customary climb out of the village up onto the clifftops. Instead I leave Coverack on a path that is only just above sea level and is flat and easy going. The sea dappled-with-light-from-above gently laps at the shoreline just a few feet below me. A short while later and the heathland style surroundings slowly morph into the (by now familiar) signs of industrial mining. This time however, I'm entering a stretch where the industry is still very much thriving. Gone are the atmospheric ruins of chimneys and abandoned caves, replaced now by the mechanical sights and sounds of a working quarry. The path is still relatively level and I'm making good early progress.

Before long I've reached the beach belonging to the hamlet of Porthoustock. The otherwise picturesque and typical Cornish beach is completely dominated by a giant concrete stone mill. A vast Orwellian rectangle that renders it completely impossible to notice anything else in the surrounding area. One of those structures that is so hideous and looming that it almost becomes beautiful. Although not quite, in this case. I now undertake the first steep climb of the day, in order to leave Porthoustock and begin an inland section of walking that Rolly says will last the next few miles. I follow this diversion across farmland and up country-lanes before catching the very welcome sight of the sea again, as I approach Porthallow.

Porthallow is an old and pretty fishing village without any noticeable giant dystopian monstrosities. Apparently, there is a rich history of pilchard fishing in this area and the village is home to a highly recommended pub, that contains many relics from this bygone era. Had I not still got so far to travel today I would doubtless stick my head around the door for a quick gander and maybe a little something to quench the old thirst. Alas, not today. As I reach Nare Point the views in front of me open up and I'm struck by the difference in scenery to that of the previous days and weeks. The rocky cliffs and turquoise (last time I promise you) seas of North Cornwall now seem as far away as the windswept isolation of North Devon and Exmoor. A lush green landscape of rich woodlands and blooming flowers stretches off into infinity ahead of me. The sea has changed too; the surfers have been replaced by sailboats and bright blues and turquoises (D'oh!) by a rich summery pale blue blanket of water. How much of this is down to the changing of the season I don't know, but the difference only serves to enrich the overall experience of walking this wondrous coastline.

I pass through the sub-tropical splendour of the Gillian Estuary as the path returns to the lazy gentility of earlier in the day. It winds in and out of thick woodland sections, giving glimpses of a distant lighthouse ahead. I come to a beautiful and intensely peaceful spot at St Anthony-in-Meneage. A tiny fishing cove with a disproportionate but splendid Norman church. A little while later, as the Helford Estuary nears, I stop for lunch in the warmth of the midday sun. After finishing off the good old processed spicy sausage snack, I reach into the pocket of my bag which contains therein my stash of sacred Mars Bars, only to find it empty. I look down at the dried mud, dust and sweat that covers my increasingly loose-fitting clothing. I decide there and then that a third rest/wash day is order tomorrow in Falmouth. I'm the master of my own destiny dear reader, never let it be said otherwise.

An hour or so later I arrive at the crossing point along the estuary. I join a small rabble of folks awaiting the Helford ferry, which is actually a small fishing boat with the word FERRY written on it in big letters. I clamber aboard with my backpack again taking up an additional space, to the delight of all concerned. The lack of eye contact from any of my fellow passengers adds further credence to my excellent plan regards finding a launderette as soon as possible. The crossing is calm and serene, gently winding in and out of floating lifeless sail boats.

The walk back along the other side of the estuary is more of the same gentle stroll through rich green woodlands. Indeed, the track continues to meander through the trees and across the occasional stretch of open farmland or secluded cove all the way to Maenporth. During this stretch I pass through the famous Trebah beach, where the Americans set off for Omaha Beach in Normandy in June 1944. I also enjoy some excellent views in both directions around Rosemullian Head.

It's around Maenporth that I meet a group of three women out for a day's hike. We walk together for a short while and swap a few stories. They are walking the ten miles from Helford to Falmouth and are shocked to hear of my 23-mile jaunt. I say shocked rather than impressed, as I do detect an undercurrent of disapproval. Indeed, a conclusion I'm reaching for myself is that any walk along this coast of longer than about

16 miles is a bit of a wasted day. You're going to miss a good deal and impress nobody. That being said – I do point out in my defence that it has been an unusually easy-going day thus far. I also take the opportunity to ask them about basking sharks and, more specifically, why I haven't seen any yet. They have no answer for me and put further strain on our fledgling relationship by proclaiming their astonishment at hearing that I've only got one confirmed seal sighting.

Some while later the imposing sight of Pendennis Castle comes into view. A spectacular sight it is too; standing triumphant against the clear blue sky, atop the cliffs. It remains in view as I continue on my way past Gyllyngvase beach, Swanpool nature reserve and then on to Pendennis Point. I test my recent theory vis-a-vis the constant unfolding drama playing out above us and look upwards. Sure enough, through the blinding sunlight, scores of gulls are swooping and crisscrossing each other at speed. It looks like a well-choreographed and painstakingly rehearsed performance as they survey all below them at a breakneck pace. I'm conscious of entering a section of coastline where sightings of birds of prey, such as the graceful buzzards and hovering kestrels, may be few and far between when compared with recent weeks. This is surely in part due to the increased numbers of people inhabiting the affluent south coast. Yet my spirits are brightened by the idea that this will also mean increased numbers of gulls in search of whatever morsels we, the most wasteful of the species, may discard. The character of these birds endears itself to me more with each passing day.

As I finally make the long haul into Falmouth my feet are screaming at me once again. This apart however, I'm in pretty good shape and am still capable of taking in the picturesque bustle of the harbour town. Hundreds of sailboats and yachts fill the harbourside as crowds of holidaymakers and residents contentedly browse the narrow streets. I have again plumped for a hotel geared towards the party pensioners market. Which again proves fruitful as I pick up a single room for two nights, overlooking the sea, at a bargain basement price. All I have to do is look unabashed at the questioning glances of the hotel staff which, to be honest with you, I'm not finding to be a problem.

That evening I take a trip to the cinema to watch the Eddie the Eagle Edwards biopic. When he said that he wanted to ski jump in the Olympics they laughed at him. An impossible task they said. His plucky heroism and gritty determination led him on a life-changing journey of discovery and ultimate success in the face of adversity. Sure, his scores may not have been as strong as those of his competitors... but he did it. I mean, come on reader, the similarities are staring you in the face here. I'm saying I'm an unlikely and loveable hero. A national treasure. I'm thinking Ryan Gosling will probably play me in the biopic. The voice of Stephen Fry could be Rolly. Writes itself.

I won't bore you with a detailed account of my third rest day, but there are a few points worthy of note before we continue. Compeed, remember that? Well according to numerous reviews on the internet it is every bit as effective as I was advised, but upon finding some I decided I'm too tight to pay for it. Feet be damned. Therefore, it's off the table so you can forget it again. Apologies to my breakfast companion back in Crackington Haven. Also (apparently) I've missed the statue that marks the half way point of the whole South West Coast Path at some point over the last few days. It's as big as me and is sat right on the path itself – and I walked past it, completely oblivious. Other than that, I rejuvenate the attire and stock up on supplies. Then spend the rest of the day wishing I was back out on the trail again. Oh, and Rolly 2 is dead, long live Rolly 3. I say a few words and leave him in the bin of my hotel room. It's all very emotional.

The following morning begins with two ferry crossings in quick succession. The first from Falmouth to St Mawes and then a shorter one across to Place, which leads on to St Anthony's Head. The experience is completely successful in terms of ridding me of any lingering enjoyment regards the novelty of river crossings. On account of me being a brave Indiana Jones/Eddie the Eagle type hero figure, I decide I don't need to trouble myself with such trifling trivialities as ferry crossing timetables. Roughly translated; I spend hours standing waiting for the blasted ferries and don't reach Place until it's nearly lunchtime; with the whole day's walk still ahead of me.

Undeterred by this shambolic start I walk on past St Anthony's Head lighthouse. An impressive brilliant white structure that was erected to warn ships of the dangers of the Manacles Rocks, some way offshore. But vastly more important to anyone of my generation for being the lighthouse that features in the opening credits of Fraggle Rock. The path continues its easy-going sprawl of the previous day, but Rolly advises me it will get a good deal tougher before the day is done. The clear warm weather of the previous few days also continues unchanged as the calm, sleepy sea sparkles below me.

What is different however is the endless stream of people. Not just in the countless sailboats out at sea, but everywhere. The path is heaving with them. It's a bank holiday Monday and as a result I'm sharing the trail with more people in any given one-hour period than I've encountered on the whole trip thus far. This continues past the positively rammed Towan beach and onto the village of Portscatho. I consider stopping for lunch here but then remember that I will shortly pass the infamous Hidden Hut. A restaurant in a small hut, specialising in fresh fish and situated on the path itself, at which Pops has eaten in the past and insists I visit on my way through. Eventually when I do find it there is a queue of people a mile long. Turns out it's more famous than infamous. I take a peek at the menu board to discover that they've run out of fish and are now only serving cups of soup at £5 a time. I've been exceptionally lucky with my timing on this trip so far, but today is definitely going some way to undoing that. I regrettably carry on past the hut without partaking of any culinary delights.

I continue past the equally crowded Pendower Beach and on to Nare Head. The crowds finally thin a touch here as the path gets slightly more challenging. The next stretch between Nare Head and Portloe contains several ups and downs that tire me out, but ultimately put a smile back on my face after what has been a cumbersome day. From Portloe I must take a walk inland to my destination for the night; the village of Veryan. The prices in Portloe are way above my budget, which I'm thinking I may find happening more and more now, as I've hit both the start of the summer season and the affluent south coast at the same time. So, I'm in a small B&B in Veryan, which is a very pretty village with two distinctive round houses at its centre. These circular cottages were built by a religious family to protect the village from the Devil, as there would be no corners for him to hide in.

The owners of the B&B are incredibly friendly and welcoming. I put aside all thoughts of art deco door stops in the dead of night and take a shower and relax for a while in my room. Later that evening I amble over to the village pub for dinner. I'm a good few miles off the path and the pub is different to any I've frequented up to now. It's an actual village pub with a few locals propping up the bar and a pleasingly simple food menu. Everyone knows each other and after the busy bank holiday walking of earlier, it's exactly what I need.

Once the chips and a pint of ale have been dispatched I call the folks and then Tasha. She is standing in the upcoming local council elections for the Green Party and is rushed off her feet with campaigning, as well as her paid employment and enforced rabbit-caring duties. I always knew I would be absent throughout the campaign due to this walk, but I feel more than a pang of guilt listening to her trying to be interested as I waffle on about overpriced soup and not seeing any basking sharks. I want to tell her that I miss her and that I wish I was there to help her and that, above all else, I am so unwaveringly proud of her for having the courage to stand up and fight for what she believes in. Instead I think I say something about the nice man in the B&B murdering me with lentil moussaka.

The next morning at breakfast I meet the inhabitants of the other guest bedroom. A pleasant couple somewhere around middle age, both with an enthusiasm for Weetabix that rivals my own. This momentarily fazes the chatty owners as we advise them we won't require any cooked breakfast but do you have any more of the aforementioned wheat-based treats? The woman is German and is therefore able to answer a question for me that has been bubbling under the surface for some time. I've noticed over the last week or so that there seems to be a disproportionate number of German (or at least German speaking) walkers on the path. She tells me that there is a long running TV programme in Germany that is set in and shot on the south Cornwall coast. The show is hugely popular amongst a certain demographic and every year hundreds of fans flock to the UK in pilgrimage, just to catch sight of the locations they've been watching on TV. She is keen to point out that she thinks the programme is a load of old tosh. Armed with this new knowledge and full-to-bursting with Weetabix goodness, I say my goodbyes and set off for today's 14-mile trek to Mevagissey.

After an uneventful trek back to the coast of a mile or so, I pick up the path coming out of Portloe. The day is warm and close but there are storms brewing over the ocean, as layers of dark clouds gather and begin to rumble. The sea itself is too calm for there not to be something major in the offing. It has turned an almost smoky grey-blue colour and its silence is deafening. Even the gulls are keeping their beaks shut as they glide overhead. There appears a purposefulness to their flight that leads me to believe they are hastily heading for cover. The path is rocky and undulating and by the time the first drops of rain land on my skin they are mingled with a layer of sweat.

As I approach Hemmick Beach the climbs become tougher and steeper and the skies darker, as the storm intensifies. There are occasional flashes of neon, jagged lightning on the horizon where sea meets sky. The scene is so staggeringly beautiful I feel as though I might explode. The power and grandeur of nature creates the sensation that I'm at the edge of everything that has ever been; the very beginning or the very end of time, of life, of all. Then - a short while later - as I approach Dodman Point the storm stops dead. The thunder and lightning vanish; taking the rain with them and the clouds part to reveal the warm bright sun smiling behind them.

With this new clarity appears some fantastic views in every direction as the path continues to wind dramatically onwards. The silence has been broken out at sea as well, as the constant lapping of the waves underpins the squawks of the newly confident gulls. The speed at which the scene before me has altered gives the storm a forgotten-dream-like quality and I momentarily wonder if it really even happened. Over the next few miles the walking continues to be challenging, but with consistent visual pay offs. Then - as I reach Gorran Haven where I'll stop for lunch - I have to negotiate some road walking.

When faced with these occasional unwelcome forays onto the tarmac, where boredom and peril collide, I tend to switch off and run on autopilot. A few minutes in and I realise that I'm chanting something over and over again under my breath, as though I'm repeating a mantra. 'Boots, boots, boots, boots,

boots, boots, boots, stick'em on your boot stumps, BOOTS!' I don't know if this is a *thing* amongst all walkers or a peculiarity singular to my increasingly fragile brain; but I've noticed it a good deal recently. A few random lines get stuck in my head and, subconsciously, I spend hours just quietly repeating them over and over again. It can be a song lyric or in some cases a new idea for my aforementioned album of rambling classics. (I'm currently working on a version of Going Loco Down in Acapulco by the Four Tops, or was it Phil Collins? Doesn't matter. It goes 'Going Coastal down in....' that's where it stops as I've yet to pass through anywhere that sounds like Acapulco. Fingers crossed.) The other day for example, I was inadvertently repeating the phrase 'In spite of what you've been told about Elvis, the good die old and helpless,' which is (of course) the opening line from a classic Carter USM song. If you're out walking in the middle of nowhere and you pass by some leathery looking chap on his own chanting 'In spite of what you've been told about Elvis, the good die old and helpless' over and over again; well it will give you a pretty sizable case of the spooks to say the least. Especially in the unlikely event that you aren't up to speed with the back catalogue of the greatest rock'n'roll band in musical history. I take a mental note, to make a conscious effort to keep this new habit in check from here on in.

Sometime later and the path has flattened out as I begin the long approach to Chapel Point. The views are as mesmerising as they've been all day and, in the warm afternoon sunshine, my face resumes the look of smug contentment that it has had for so much of this adventure so far. As I slowly descend through rolling green farmland the buildings that populate Chapel Point come into view. A small group of white 1930s style houses clumped together in this idyllic and isolated spot. It's duly added to the ever-growing list of places along this coastline that I'm definitely going to live in when a sack of money falls from the sky into my lap.

I pass through the attractive Portmellon Beach, littered with families out exploring rock pools and chomping ice creams. Then my destination for the day at last appears in the distance. Mevagissey (not 'Megavissy' as I'm continually referring to it) is a pretty and busy fishing village complete with working harbour and typical picture postcard Cornish cottages. I'm booked into a hotel that sits atop a hill way above the village, with its bustling narrow streets. Once I've checked in and showered I explore the crowded alleyways in search of sustenance. I eventually settle for a chippy by the harbourside and sit on a bench overlooking the sea. I share my meal with a grateful and somewhat shabby looking gull. When we're both full we sit and watch the world go by for a while, in the fading light.

The following morning I'm sat in the classy period décor dining room of the hotel, chewing happily on the old bix of Weet. I glance up and notice that the male half of the couple sat two tables along from mine is Shakin' Stevens. Now, I know what you're thinking dear reader. Come on Reynolds, I hear you cry, are you expecting us to believe that you've seen Enfield and Stevens, on the same trip? To which I reply; don't forget the café in St Ives where I may or may not have been sitting within reach of a former Blue Peter presenter.

We need to talk about Rolly. I'm packing up my kit a short while later and decide I can no longer ignore the inconvenient truth. This latest regeneration of my earnest walking companion is a touch left field for my pallet. Quick referencing no longer seems possible as he rumbles endlessly on with detailed history lessons and nearby sites of interest. Worst of all the sections are no longer split into day length walks. What all of this means, dear reader, is that I have to think for myself. To quote Wodehouse this leaves me, if not absolutely disgruntled, then certainly a good deal less than gruntled. I eye him disapprovingly and shove him into a side pocket in my backpack. I can only hope he comes to his senses sooner rather than later because I'm not an idiot, as you know, and as it stands he's of no more use to me than my tent, sleeping bag, roll mat and.... well let's just say the vast majority of things I'm hauling around on my back.

The weather is warm but drizzly as I leave Mevagissey. The first signs of just how tough today's 17-mile hike to Fowey is going to be arrive within minutes. Viciously steep climbs in quick succession leave me struggling for breath before my Weetabix have even settled. The sweeping views of undulating hills stretching off into the distance bring with them the realisation that these sharp ascents and descents are going to be the predominant feature of the day.

A few miles in I encounter a small group of half a dozen or so sheep. They are clearly escapees from a nearby farm, now perched precariously on the cliff edge, chomping merrily away on the forbidden flora. I try to edge past them without spooking them. This doesn't work and as soon as they spy me they scarper off along the path. For the following thirty minutes, I'm essentially shepherding them along the narrow, winding track. I try to appeal to their sense of reason. 'Look just let me pass you idiots, I have no desire to be arrested for livestock theft.' This falls on deaf ears and I'm starting to contemplate the idea of arriving in Fowey this afternoon with a small flock of sheep in tow, when the path finally widens. This empowers them to pluck up enough courage to stand trembling in a small clearing and let me pass. To the nearby farmer missing half a dozen of their sheep; I'm sorry, I did everything I could under the circumstances.

Shortly thereafter the path is becoming rockier and even more exhausting. The views on to Charlestown are outstanding through the continued light drizzle. As I reach the stunning

Black Head Rock, a buzzard circles overhead and I allow myself five minutes to watch in awe as the graceful bird soars, hovers and swoops, in search of a spot of brunch. Black Head is the site of an old Iron Age fort and is a perfect example of this stretch of coastline at its very best. I continue on my way into Charlestown where I stop for a very welcome lunch. This attractive town is rich in history with beautiful old-fashioned ships anchored in its authentic harbour. It was also used as a location to film the famous motion picture 'The Eagle Has Landed.' So, plenty for me to mull over as I wolf down the old MB.

Any hopes I had of an easier afternoon are soon dashed as I enter a section of path referred to locally as the Cornish Alps. The views are as stunning as the walking is back breaking. By the time I reach Par and the impressive Par Sands beach I'm very nearly spent. An inland section follows as I negotiate the river Par. On this occasion I'm glad of it, as it brings with it a mercifully flat stretch of path that follows a local cycle track. This turns out to be relatively short-lived however, and the rocky climbs soon resume. Rising to windswept headlands and descending down through rich woodland into picturesque, hidden coves.

I pass the striking red and white striped tower at Gribbin Head. I have no idea what it is or was used for but it's a pretty, if slightly comical, addition to the luscious coastline in this section. I continue past a beach marked as private. This section of the south coast has many such private beaches. It's a concept alien to me, I didn't realise you could even own a beach. It doesn't sit easy with me if I'm being honest but, on this occasion, it does bring with it a family of swans relaxing at the water's edge. I stand and watch them for a few minutes before dragging my aching legs onwards.

I reach Fowey utterly exhausted with the rain still drizzling down, as it has been all day. I'm booked into a pub sat on the harbourside for the evening. The bustling town gives me a strong sense of deja-vu, so similar is the scene to that of the previous evening, albeit on a larger scale. There can be no doubt that holiday season is now in full swing, as each location I arrive at is full to the brim with happy tourists, lapping up the delights of these Cornish coastal resorts. So tired am I from the day's exertions that the evening is spent in the pub below my room sipping the local ale, writing up my notes from the last few days and chatting to the friendly bar staff. They tell me about some of the places I'll walk through over the next couple of days and I go to bed tipsy with excitement for what lies ahead.

As I set off the next morning the sun is bright and warm and the twelve-mile walk to Looe promises much. The day begins with another ferry crossing from Fowey to Polruan. Whilst I'm waiting I get chatting to a chap who's about to be picked up for work. He's a construction worker and is initially bewildered and a touch derogatory when I tell him about the journey I've embarked on. By the time his lift arrives however, he concedes that he wishes he was coming with me and shakes me by the hand, before being driven away. I briefly contemplate the reactions I've had from the many folks I've met along the way. It can be said that there is rarely a middle ground. Either they think I'm a total moron for voluntarily walking 630 miles on my own, when there are perfectly good public transport options available. Or they are jealous of the adventure I'm on and wish they could join me on it. It seems it's either your idea of heaven or hell. As the small boat that is to ferry me across the river pulls up alongside me, I'm in no doubt. I wouldn't swap this adventure for all the package holidays to Majorca, stag weekends in Ibiza or gap years in Thailand that money can buy.

The next stretch from Polruan to Polperro is across land owned by the National Trust. This usually suggests some quality walking and scenery are in the offing. I'm not disappointed as I instantly pick up where I left off the previous day, with spectacular views as the single-track path winds its way around and over dramatic rocky cliffs, and through secluded woody coves. So spectacular are the views here that I can just make out the Lizard in one direction. It feels like so long ago I was there and the sight of it brings with it a wave of nostalgia. I stop this in its tracks pretty quick sharpish however, deciding it more worthwhile to focus on what's ahead of me rather than behind me.

I spy an impressive natural rock arch sticking out to sea over the cliff edge and stop to take a few pictures of it. As I do this a rabbit appears from a nearby clump of shrubbery and sits on the path in front of me. These cuddly, destructive fur balls have been a consistent addition to the landscape over the last few days. This one, however, bears all the tell-tale signs of that most vile of human-introduced diseases: myxomatosis. I've dreaded this situation; do I have the courage to put the creature out of its undoubted misery? As I watch its emaciated frame limp blindly around, in search of food, I know that I must. I pick up a suitably sized rock and attempt to creep up on it. As I do this, it hears me, hops into the shrubbery on the cliff edge and disappears. I'm saddened and relieved in equal measure.

As I carry on towards Polperro the animal encounters continue thick and fast. Fields full of sheep and cows pass by in the sweltering May sunshine. When walking I'm always nervous of large groups of cows. Such placid, peaceful creatures you may say. To which I reply; that's all well and good dear reader, but you try being chased from numerous fields by gangs of the boisterous little blighters. True, this only generally occurs when it's a field of young inquisitive males. Nonetheless, it leaves its mark on even the bravest of handsome explorers, such as yours truly. So, it's with a tip-toeing caution that I pass these bovine obstacles.

As with the previous few days, the path mixes open rocky clifftop walking with stretches of dense, rich woodland. After emerging from one such stretch I begin the approach to the idyllic village of Polperro. I pass a striking First World War memorial during my descent. Polperro shares its basic traits with the majority of Cornish harbour villages I've passed through since Lands' End, but it's a particularly pretty example of such. I make my way through the crowds of tourists that fill its steep narrow walkways. Once I've reached the other side and the crowds have cleared, I pick a spot and stop for lunch. Unwrapping the MB of the day I sit and watch the sea gently lap at the shoreline below me. The gulls begin to eye me excitedly from above and, when they start circling closer, I take it as a sign and get on my way. Everybody likes Mars Bars.

More steep climbs follow and I'm again struggling by the time I reach Talland Bay. The Church on one side of the bay is arrestingly placed for maximum effect. I use this as an excuse to rest up for a few minutes and sit taking in the vista, imagining how dramatic this scene would look on a dark stormy evening. From here on, the remaining few miles to Looe are a bit easier on the old leg muscles. I've booked into a cheap hotel for the night. Something I'm exceptionally grateful for, as the recent hike in prices is doing some serious damage to my daily budget and the prospect of the canvas is once again looming. The town of Looe is split into two very distinctive sections; West Looe and East Looe. My hotel is in the former, which appears to be the quieter of the two, with the main town itself being in East Looe.

My hotel stands out amongst the posh B&Bs, guesthouses and more upmarket hotels that adorn the streets along the promenade. If it was in Shoreditch it would be called shabby chic; it isn't though... in Shoreditch I mean. It's in West Looe. I arrive at reception and ring the bell. A small King Charles Spaniel appears in answer to my call and lies down on its back in front of me, awaiting the presumed belly rub. From this moment on I fall in love with the place. Its Kubrick-esque décor wins me over. 1970s style paintings of glamourous women in pastel colours adorn the walls, and I think the carpet actually is the same as the one as in The Shining.

After a while the proprietor arrives and affords me a friendly welcome. A tall man in large, square, orange-tinted spectacles and a green polo shirt, proudly emblazoned with the hotel's name. He is as eccentric as his domain suggests and mentions the hotel's excellent balcony and garden facilities at least twenty times whilst showing me to my room. I tell him I'm in love with his dog and he replies that everybody is.

'She's a tart, but I'm fond of her.'

After unpacking I leave my room to discover the dog sitting patiently outside my door. As soon as she sees me she rolls over again, expectantly.

'You really are a tart,' I say, as I make a fuss of her.

I take the 15-minute walk along the quayside into East Looe for dinner. After dining on a cheese and jalapeno wrap and chips, (I really need to work on the diet) I return to the hotel and make my way to the bar. There are a few other guests dotted around as I take a seat by the window. Soon the proprietor, who seems to run the place single-handed, reappears and takes my drinks order. He chats enthusiastically to all the guests, myself included, and tells me again about the balcony and garden facilities. I duly retire, drink in hand, to the much-hyped balcony area, where I lazily sit and look out to sea. For the record, it is a lovely balcony, this cannot be denied.

The next morning at breakfast, again served by the proprietor himself, I'm consulting Rolly regards the day ahead. A short eight-mile jaunt to the excellently named Port Wrinkle. I'm chuckling to myself, mainly at the word wrinkle, when the proprietor materialises beside me with a small silver tray filled with Dairylea triangles. I look at him, obviously visibly confused.

'For your toast?'

'Oh, I see. No that's fine thanks, I'll just be having some Weetabix.' I can see he is hurt by this news.

'Are you sure? We have a full cooked breakfast on the menu... you can eat it on the balcony if you like... or in the garden?'

'No, no that's fine, thank you very much though.' He is still looking crest-fallen and in the end, not wanting to hurt the man's feelings, we agree on a compromise and I take a Dairylea triangle.

It's with some regret that I leave the hotel behind me and set off on my way. You would struggle to find a more welcoming and enjoyable place to stay in this part of the world. I vow to leave a good review on TripAdvisor as I begin the day's walk with a stroll back through East Looe and into the woodlands beyond it. The day is blisteringly hot and so the shade of the trees is a welcome start. I pass through Millendreath village as the views open up. A handful of the customary steep climbs follow soon after, before I reach the heights of the impressive Bodigga Cliffs.

An area of coastal erosion means I'm diverted inland for a stretch. This leads down some pleasant country lanes before I rejoin the path again. I see a group of gliders ahead of me and stop for lunch to watch them in flight. The participants are clearly revelling in the experience on a clear, hot day over the sparkling sea. I watch as the gulls give them a wide berth whilst eyeing them curiously. Once I've consumed the good old rations I apply generous amounts of Sudocrem to my ankles, shoulders and a few of my more personal areas. I apologise for so abruptly bringing down the tone, dear reader, but I feel it's important I relay to you the complete experience, warts and all. (Please note: I don't have warts. In any areas;

personal or otherwise.) The rise in temperature, coupled with the sustained tough walking of the last week or so, have brought with them a good deal of unwelcome chafing.

The path continues to undulate until I reach the Battern Cliffs, which Rolly advises (I can't stay mad at him) are some of the highest on the south coast. I can see the path continuing along the clifftop in front of me and carry on with a spring in my step. The walking here is fantastic; the bright sunshine, clear blue skies and reflective beauty of the ocean below leave me in an almost meditative state. The gulls swoop silently above me and for the first time today there is not another soul in sight. I walk through some small residential areas and have the sense of stepping back in time. Tiny - seemingly deserted - hamlets that would have looked almost identical a hundred years ago to how they do today.

As today's walk is only eight miles long I'm soon approaching Port Wrinkle. I look at my notes and see that my hotel is on Finnygook Lane. Nearby on the map is the small village of Crafthole. I'm staying on Finnygook Lane, in Port Wrinkle, just outside Crafthole. Perhaps I've been alone too long, but this is all too much for me and I'm overcome with fits of laughter. After calming down I decide that I will definitely start using the word Crafthole as a derogatory term. You are a complete Crafthole. That guy, oh, he's a total Crafthole. That sort of thing.

I'm staying at the only hotel in Port Wrinkle. It's a Victorian building on a grand old scale and is full to the brim with holidaymakers. This is fairly surreal as the rest of this sleepy spot is empty and the hotel is a sharp contrast to the isolation of the last few hours. Yours truly is once again in the bargain 'backpackers' room, tucked safely away from the rest of the guests. My budget won't stretch to a meal at the hotel's restaurant and so I wander down the beach to a small hut I passed on the way in serving chips, which makes a nice change. That night I'm sat in my room contemplating the next few days. My old mate Mickey B is going to come out and meet me in Plymouth to walk a day or two with me. However, I've mistimed my arrival to the city and as a result am faced with the prospect of three nights there. Mickey B has already booked his B&B and is travelling a fair old distance to visit me, so there's no scope for changing the arrangements. Worse things have happened at sea, but nevertheless, I'm not looking forward to being off the trail for so long.

I set off early the following morning for the 15-mile walk to Plymouth. Rolly seems to suggest that the walk is a fairly moderate one. As I say, he's not as direct as he once was, but this seems to be what he's getting at. Before I even leave Port Wrinkle I'm faced with crossing a golf course. Have I mentioned I'm not a huge fan? Thankfully golfers as a breed are legendarily lazy by nature and so I'm past the course before any of them have so much as brushed their teeth. If they even brush their teeth. Probably not, golfers as a breed have notoriously bad teeth. I've also heard it was golfers that introduced grey squirrels into our countryside and in doing so wiped out the native red squirrel. Don't shoot the messenger, I'm just telling you what I've heard. (Note: Golfers did not introduce grey squirrels to the UK. Or did they? No.)

After negotiating the golf course I'm faced with a military firing range. The red flags are flying, which means I must spend the next few miles walking on a pavement by the side of a road. I've heard that the number one leisure pursuit for retired members of the armed forces is golf. This isn't as unpleasant as it could be as I still enjoy great views out to sea, and the early hour means next to no traffic on the road. Plus, I use this time to work on my album of walking classics. Porthcurno almost works; 'Going loco down in Porthcurno, I've been gone too long.'

When I return to the coast the path delivers the first inspired stretch of walking of the day. Apart from a number of unattractive clusters of mobile holiday homes, the views are spectacular and the trail is winding and challenging. I'm joined by large numbers of crows, who seem to have wrestled control of this stretch of coastline from the usually dominant gulls. They gracefully glide beside me, just out to sea, occasionally disappearing from view below the cliff edge. The sticky heat has brought with it armies of bugs that buzz around me in swarms, like living clouds. Every now and then one will fly, kamikaze style, into my eye or mouth and I spend a good deal of time rubbing my eyes and spluttering.

I pass over the beautiful and seemingly endless Whitsand Bay. This whole area is adorned with Dartmoor ponies, grazing on the hillsides and strolling past with no interest in me whatsoever. Next, I reach Rame Head and stop to sit a while and drink in the views out across the deep blue sea. The flowers are out in force, dotted all over the rocky landscape and completing the rich, warm summer feel of the day. After about ten minutes I decide to plough on, as it would be very easy to nod off here and I've still got a fair few miles ahead of me.

From there on in the path starts to get a good deal less rugged. After rounding Rame Head I'm on the approach to Plymouth and passing through areas of managed woodland and park. The path becomes decidedly manicured and more and more people begin to appear with pushchairs and picnic baskets, enjoying the glorious sunshine. The spectre of Plymouth is soon visible in the distance ahead. A vast smoking metropolis through an increasingly thick muggy heat-haze. It's a strange sight. I live in a city probably five times the size of Plymouth and yet, at this moment, it could be London or New York. It's far and away the largest urban expanse I've seen in the last six weeks and I would be lying if I said it was anything other than a completely unwelcome sight.

As I get ever nearer to the sprawling concrete jungle I'm hit by the feeling of walking back to reality. I've not been in anything approaching real isolation since arriving on the south coast, but Plymouth is not a holiday town or pretty fishing village. It's a real city where people live out their lives working in offices and shops, where there is homelessness and decay, cinema's and bowling alleys. Where there are fights outside pubs and parking tickets. Where there are double bacon cheeseburgers and pound shops. In short, the real world, where I live, work in an office, eat double bacon cheeseburgers and go to the cinema.

Eventually I reach Cawsand, where I catch the ferry across into Plymouth itself. It's hot and densely populated but, in truth, far from being the ugliest of cities. My hotel is a trendy converted townhouse that is affordable, mainly because it's only just opened. I check into the room that I'll spend the next three nights in and attempt to formulate a plan to see me through, until I can rejoin the trail. There is a stretch of the Coast Path itself that goes through the city centre. So, if I walk that tomorrow then when Mickey B arrives we won't need to spend any time in the city and can pick up the trail from the other side of Plymouth. There's also all the usual laundry and stocking up of supplies to be done.

Lastly, I have some friends who live in nearby Totnes. I've planned to meet up with them a week or so from now when I'm passing through Brixham. So, it seems sensible to see if they're about and pay them a visit over the next few days as well. It's all starting to sound manageable and my spirits are rising. I make the call and arrange to catch the train to Totnes and meet them tomorrow. I then call the folks, Tasha and my brother before heading out to grab some food.

Sophy and Dan are a couple that used to live near us in Bristol. They were good friends of ours, until they decided to betray us forever by upping sticks and moving to the countryside. Thereby leaving us to fend for ourselves and revealing themselves to be selfish, mean-spirited people, who probably now play golf. Sophy used to work with Tasha, which is how we all met. Dan used to be a chef and now, together, they run their own successful bakery in Totnes. It's called the Almond Thief and you should all go and visit it as its ruddy marvellous. Although, as I say they are the type of people that leave their friends for dead at the drop of a hat… award winning sourdough loaves notwithstanding.

It's great to catch up with them and their young son Ezra (who may have spent his entire life coping with being named Moses were it not for yours truly, but that's another story). We have a few beers, Dan cooks a fantastic barbecue and I then share with them my 500 photographs of the sea. I also get to meet Sophy's Mum who they're currently sharing a house with and her beautiful and soppy old sheepdog Bill. We agree some vague plans to meet up again in a few days' time when I reach the Brixham area and a thoroughly good time is had by all.

The second day in Plymouth is spent walking the urban stretch of the Coast Path across the city. Halfway round I buy lunch and spend a pleasant hour or so basking in the sun on the common, by the lighthouse, looking out to sea. This is followed in the afternoon by the launderette and food shopping. The day is rounded off by a visit to a Mexican restaurant followed by the quietest pub I could find. All in all, being stranded in Plymouth isn't as terrible as it first appeared. That being said, I'm foaming at the mouth to get out of the ruddy place and back to the Coast Path. With Plymouth comes the passing from South Cornwall to South Devon. When I get going again tomorrow, I'll be back in the county where it all began. Apart from I won't… Because the path technically starts in Somerset. Which ruins that previous sentence. Which is a shame, because it was a great sentence… Full of atmosphere and meaning… a really good way to end this section. Shame.

4. South & East Devon

Vegetarians from Barnsley, Luxury Spa Retreats and Pop's Swansong.

I arrive at Plymouth coach station to meet Mickey B a full hour early the following day. I'm brimming with excitement at the prospect of getting back on the trail. He's not arriving until late morning so we've got a short eight-mile trek planned to Wembury, where I'll find a campsite and he'll catch the bus back to his B&B in Plymouth. He'll then get the first bus back to Wembury the following day to meet me, walk half the day's hike with me and then head back to Wembury to get the bus back to Plymouth again. Yes, I know; I've had three nights in Plymouth to reach the conclusion that between the two of us we, maybe, could have planned this better.

Eventually I spy his smiling, baldy northern head, from the window of an arriving coach. Mickey B is an old and dear friend whom I first met when we worked together many years ago, down in Brighton. He and his equally lovely, but much less northern, partner Hayley have recently moved to Bristol, just down the road from us in fact. When I first knew him, he was a Techno loving clubber in his early thirties who loved a drink or five. Today he's a teetotal vegetarian in his forties who loves a lime cordial, as long as it's a half. Time: a cruel and fickle mistress. Of course, I'm one to talk; I'm an ale drinker on a walking holiday. It catches up with us all dear reader. We greet each other with much cordiality and I thank him sincerely for taking the trouble to come all that way to walk with me. It's a joy to see the old codger again.

The first stretch of the day's walk is urban and unpleasant, as we negotiate our way through the east side of Plymouth. We cross the bridge at Billacombe road, alongside the constant stream of traffic and on through Oreston, where we get lost several times. Eventually we arrive at the attractive but absolutely heaving harbour development in the run up to Mount Batten Point. We stop at a pub overlooking the water for a lavish Sunday Roast with all the trimmings. Well, I do. Mickey B's plate consists mainly of broccoli and swede I think. Then, with our bellies suitably inflated, we push on. There is a complicated bit of navigation soon afterwards where we lose the waymarkers for a spell. I then spot one over the other side of the road and we appear to pass through the tricky patch unscathed.

A short while on and Rolly is causing me confusion. We should have passed Mount Batten Tower by now and our direction of travel doesn't make sense against what I'm looking at on the map. I consult Mickey B and he stares at me questioningly. 'Yeah well, we missed that bit out didn't we' he says, pointing at Mount Batten Point on the map. 'What do you mean?' I ask, trying to remain cool and collected. 'Yeah back there when it got confusing, you spotted the sign at the other side of the road and we picked it up, skipping this loop out here.' I looked back at him in astonishment. 'Why didn't you say something?' 'Oh, I thought it were deliberate, I thought you knew.' So, there it is dear reader. A half a mile stretch of the South West Coast Path that I missed out. All the times in my future when I tell people I've walked the whole of this mammoth trail I will, in fact, be lying. All thanks to a teetotal vegetarian from Barnsley. And if you're reading this thinking that it sounds like it was me that picked the wrong route and it's therefore my fault... well you can shut up as well. You idiot.

The sun is beating down on us as we finally leave the urban sprawl behind us and reach open fields. The path winds gently up and down for a long stretch with no major climbs to tire us out. We pass the time by chatting about everything from the footy results to house prices in the south west. Inevitably, I spend a good deal of time telling stories from the trip so far; the best sections of walking, the places I've stayed and the people I've met. Eventually talk turns to my diet. I may, from time to time, throw the odd gentle jest in Mickey B's direction re the old zero flesh lifestyle choice. The truth is however that his decision to be a vegetarian is based on strong and sound ethical grounds and is to be admired. For my part, I've always made a point of attempting to limit my meat consumption to free range products – and here we get to the nub of the issue. I've been merrily chomping on processed sausage snacks, dodgy burgers and cheap chicken wraps (no pun intended) throughout the whole walk so far. Upon hearing this my old friend, with no more than an understated but stern raise of the eyebrow, conveys that this makes me a hypocritical, low life douchebag with the murderous morals of a fascist war criminal. A smidge strong perhaps, but I'm suitably ashamed and vow to address the situation.

The going continues to be gentle and relatively flat. This is fortunate, as I'm remembering very clearly now what the major issue is with going walking with Mickey B. He moves at 40 million miles an hour. He is an experienced long-distance walker and, fuelled by all those cauliflowers and mange tout, he is a man on a mission. I repeatedly point out to him that I'm carrying a backpack heavier than an artic lorry, but he only seems to be able to retain this information for about three minutes at a time. This elaborate routine continues past the pretty bays of Jennycliff, Leekbed and Crownhill, as the sea remains silent and still in the hot afternoon sunshine. I point out, subtly and breezily of course, that this easy flat walking is not indicative of the trail as a whole. I wouldn't want there to be any confusion regards the level of heroism I've displayed to get this far.

Somewhere past the beautiful Wembury Point we stop for some liquid refreshment, at a pub just off the trail. Whilst there we get chatting to a family on the next table to ours. 'How come you're carrying a bag the size of a house and he's only got a tiny little rucksack?' One of their number enquires. 'He's from Barnsley' I quip, cleverly inventing a new and baseless stereotype in the process. After the exchanging of a few more pleasantries I reveal that I've not yet booked anywhere to stay in nearby Wembury. The lady of the family very kindly offers us the use of their guest bedroom. I detect that her husband is slightly less enthusiastic about the prospect of two random hikers staying in their house, and would like to tell you that this is the reason we politely decline. The truth however, is that after discussing the matter, we both decide we are too scared.

After leaving the pub we are back on the trail and are soon making the short inland trek to Wembury. The afternoon is still warm and the sea radiates a silky shimmering glow. When we arrive in the small, slightly nondescript, village we head straight for pub number three of the day. We've arrived later than expected, predominantly due to pub's number one and two, and I realise I've only got twenty minutes to book into the village campsite before it closes. I leave Mickey B manly sipping a lime cordial and soda through a straw and run as quickly as my aching limbs will allow. I reach it just in time and dump a few of my things before heading back to the pub. We order some dinner and talk a bit about the following days walk. A few hours later, when I'm drunk and Mickey B is in the midst of a fully-fledged, cordial induced, sugar rush, we head for the bus stop. After waving him goodbye and arranging where to meet the next morning I amble up the road to the campsite, where I do a distinctly slap dash job of putting up the old tent.

Stupid tent, I mean *seriously*, what is the point? I know I've said it before but this is absolutely the last time Mr Tent. I've had a few hours broken sleep and now here I am at the break of dawn, again attempting to shove endless miles of canvas into a bag that has definitely been swapped for a smaller one during the night. The temperature dropped in the early hours to, at most, minus a thousand degrees and I'm aching all over. It's several hours until I'm due to meet Mickey B so I decide to slowly wander towards the beach, in search of breakfast.

I purchase something loosely approximating a Danish pastry from a newsagent and amble back down the road towards the water. That first sight of the sea has an increasing sense of profoundness with every passing day. A hitherto unrealised weight is lifted the moment my eyes rest upon the seductive waves; be they silent and still, full of fury, or boisterous and playful. The feeling is more pronounced each morning and today my stroppy mood and tired lack of enthusiasm are washed away and replaced by a calm contentment. The sun is fully ablaze in the clear blue sky and my spirits are on the up as I think about the 17-mile trek to Bantham, that lies ahead of me.

Whilst I'm waiting for Mickey B I get chatting to a middle-aged lady out walking her dog; an elderly terrier that looks and moves as though it too must have spent an uncomfortable night under the canvas. We end up talking for a good thirty minutes or so. She tells me that she is a retired parole officer who has recently moved to this area to be near to her, previously estranged, son. Due to a difficult set of circumstances in her earlier life, she was left with no option but to put her child up for adoption. Many years later she went looking for him, fearing an understandable but painful rejection, but finding instead a deep and lasting bond. It's all pretty emotional stuff and by the time Mickey B's well rested and cheery noggin appears, I'm not too far off having a case of the old quivering lip. I say goodbye and wish her all the very best as Mickey B and I fall into step beside each other.

The path is flat and easy in the run up to the first of three ferry crossings during today's walk. During this opening one mile stretch, Mickey B delights in telling me how comfortable his night's rest had been and shows little or no sympathy for my tale of woe and hardship. We make the ferry crossing by the skin of our teeth; for someone that walks at a trillion miles an hour he seems to have a knack for making me late for everything. The tiny boat takes us across the River Yealm to Noss Mayo. From here we join a wide track leading us through picturesque countryside, strewn with beautiful ancient Oak trees. We follow this track along the river back towards the ocean in the warm sunshine. There are clouds beginning to gather overhead but the sea remains quiet, as the odd passing gull on surveillance duty glides by.

The walking continues to be easy going as the path clings to low grassy cliffs that roll gently down to meet the deep blue water. In the approach to Stoke Point a few miles later the views become a touch more dramatic as the wind picks up and the waves begin to quietly crash into the, now visible, jagged rocks below us. Mickey B is in his element as he strolls quicker than I can run along the single file track. We chat about the possibility of a future long-distance trail together; possibly the Pennine Way. Somewhere around Bigbury Bay the track enters an area of farmland and begins a stretch of steep climbs and slippery grassland descents. At the foot of one of these descents and with one eye on the time, Mickey B turns back. We say our goodbyes and arrange another meet up. He and Hayley are going to join Tasha and our neighbour Paddy when they come and visit me in Brixham in a few days. Sophy and Dan will also join us there, so it should be a-good-old-knees-up.

I'm sorry to see the old sod go and stand and watch as he storms off at a gazillion miles an hour back down the path, quickly disappearing from view. A fellow insomniac, Mickey

B is one of only two people I know (the other being my Pops) that truly understands the need to be a sole moving dot on a vast open landscape. Alone again, I climb the next hill as the rain begins to lightly fall. A short while later and the heavens have well and truly opened. I slip on a steep descent, fall on my backside and slide down a grassy verge. Covered in mud and soaked to the bone, I trudge on as the visibility worsens. For the second time in the last week or so I'm amazed at how quickly and completely the weather can turn along this coastline.

Later that afternoon, with the rain still pounding down, I reach the second crossing of the day at the River Erme. I need to cross this on foot as its too shallow for a boat crossing. I consult Rolly, who smugly points out that I needed to time my arrival here to just before or just after low tide. As I haven't done this, and have no idea what time low tide was/is, I walk along the river until I find a spot that 'looks' shallow. I begin to unlace my boots when I decide that this is pointless, as every inch of me is soaked through already. I lift my oversized, overweight backpack above my head and bravely take the plunge. Initially the water is only knee high and I sigh with relief, as I begin to wade across to the other side. Somewhere around half distance however, things take a turn for the worse and the water is now at waist height. As the icy cold penetrates my nether regions and panic threatens to set in I close my eyes, hope for the best, and keep going. The river reaches just above my belly before I eventually begin to rise again and press on, into shallower waters.

I reach the other side and sling down the backpack. I notice there is a couple watching me. Oh good, I'm glad there was an audience for that... who needs dignity anyway, right? They approach me and, trying not to laugh, check that I'm alright. I try my best to look cool. I aim to give the impression that I knew well in advance exactly how deep the river was, and that

I'm the sort of rugged adventurer that does this kind of thing on a daily basis. This may have been more convincing if I were able to stop shaking with cold. They kindly offer to drive me to my final destination for the day. I thank them but decline and, after emptying my boots and pointlessly ringing out my socks, I trudge comically on.

The last stretch of the walk is mercilessly tough going. The rain continues as I clamber up ever more slippery hillsides and slide back down again. The scenery, as I pass the Jagged Teeth at Westcombe beach and then Aymer Cove, is the Coast Path at its rugged best. I'm reminded of Hartland Point and the stormy beauty of North Devon but, in truth, am in no fit state to fully appreciate it. I'm barely standing by the time I reach Bigbury on Sea and the majestic Burgh Island. Ordinarily I would have stopped at least a half a dozen times over the last few miles to soak up the beauty that surrounds me. Yet, as the rain continues to lash down, I'm motivated only by the prospect of the warm and dry pub, that awaits me in Bantham.

The pub is just over the River Avon, the third and final river of the day. I have, of course, missed the last ferry crossing and so end up taking an eight-mile taxi ride. The car eventually dropping me off thirty feet across the water from where it picked me up 15 minutes earlier. But I don't care; I'm elated to have made it to my accommodation for the evening. It has been a varied and at times spectacular trek from Wembury, and I feel as though the true essence of the trail has returned. The last memories of urban Plymouth seem to have been laid to rest. I spend the evening in front of the fire in the pub recovering, before retiring to a warm bed and a sound sleep.

The next day begins with a straight choice between a still damp set of clothes or an absolutely eye wateringly stinky set, from the deepest, darkest depths of the backpack. I plump for the latter and almost instantly regret my decision. After dispensing with the chef's finest Weetabix and semi-skimmed,

I step out into the blazing hot sunshine of the new day. The damp clothes would have dried in mere seconds, whereas the heat will further intensify the potency of the already honking garments as the day progresses. Even the gulls are keeping their distance as I rejoin the path.

The walking is initially easy going as I pass through Thurlestone. To complete the smelly Stig-of-the-Dump motif I'm soon encircled by my own entourage of tiny insects. They buzz around my head with frantic purpose, oblivious to my increasingly elaborate hand waving protests. After several unpleasant minutes, the clouds of miniscule assassins clear just long enough for me to catch sight of Thurlestone golf course, sprawling out in front of me. I pass through the variety of warning signs as the early morning argyle brigade take care to avoid eye contact with the strange creature, emitting the foul stench and putting them off their swing.

Things improve dramatically as soon as I pass through the course however. As the houses disappear from the landscape, the path begins to dip and climb and the sea weighs up whether or not to muster any crashing waves, to complete the ambience. Eventually it decides it's too much effort and the remaining walk to Hope Cove is still and peaceful, through the thickening heat haze. A kestrel hovers silently in front of me, searching for a mid-morning snack. Each time I get within a certain distance of it the bird powers forward a few hundred yards to safety, then hovers once more. Initially I assume this is merely a precautionary measure but then wonder if my powerful odour has a two-hundred-yard radius.

After a short jaunt along a country lane I arrive at the pretty fishing village of Hope Cove. The grass covered rock clusters jutting out to sea contrast against the quaint cottages and, very appealing country pub, that sit behind the beachfront. The overall effect is strikingly attractive, and the height of the cliffs on either side give the whole thing a wonderfully secluded feel.

The walking continues to slowly intensify as I leave Hope Cove and the climbs become steeper and rockier. The views in both directions along this section are breath-taking. Even through the blur of the heat haze I can see far into the distance, as I break into a broad smile. Each time I get a view like this ahead of me on this trail, a childish excitement washes over me. I'm looking at the adventures of the next few days, a sneak preview. It dawns on me that when I started the walk I was forever looking backwards, amazed at how far I'd travelled, but as the trip goes on its these forward vistas that bring me the most joy. This is especially true as I enter the final third of the journey, as it provides a welcome reminder that there is still so much to look forward to.

The walking and scenery continue to deliver as I approach Bolt Head. The track thins as it clings to the hillside and the sea remains eerily calm a few hundred feet below. My feet begin to ache and the pack is feeling heavy on my back, but I'm walking at pace and with a raw enthusiasm. These last few miles between Hope Cove and Bolt Head have confirmed something I already knew to be true. The South Devon coast, at its best, is every bit as awe inspiring and beautiful as that of North Devon or Cornwall. It's just not nearly as often that you come across these unspoilt sections on the south coast. The coastline here is far more densely populated and boasts many more affluent holiday spots. All wonderful places if that's your bag, but for the walker, places like Bolt Head show you a glimpse of how phenomenal it would once have been to walk this stretch.

Speaking of affluent holiday spots, they don't come any more affluent than my destination for the night; Salcombe. The long roadside walk through the town, as well as drenching me in sweat in the hot late afternoon sunshine, allows me to gaze at the multi million pound properties, high class eateries and gigantic yachts and sailboats moored in the harbour. You know what they say; when in Rome. I have (somewhat recklessly) splashed out on the poshest hotel of the entire trip. I'm talking luxury spa retreat here. I'm in the cheapest room of course, but there's cheap and there's 'this really isn't cheap at all.' I waft into the large foyer area and, if I do say so myself, turn a few heads in the process. Nothing to do with my red-faced, sweaty appearance or penetrating odour I'm sure. Memories of my first night in Porlock Weir come back to me, as I'm hastily removed from public view and shown to my room.

I peel off the old rags and relax for an hour or two in the jacuzzi bath tub. I then wander around the vast room in my fluffy dressing gown, sipping a single malt from the mini bar, whilst perusing the dinner menu. Having decided on the charred leeks and white asparagus with hazelnuts and milk skin, I clap on the lights, switch on the fifty-inch HD flat screen and hop onto the four-poster water bed for a well-earned siesta. People just don't realise how tough the nomadic lifestyle of the long-distance walker can be.

Apparently, the hotel is too posh to have Weetabix, so I'm forced to slum it the next morning with some Eggs Florentine. Whilst I'm tucking in, a horrible elderly couple spend a full twenty minutes shouting at the lady serving breakfasts, for having the nerve to request that they sit at any table in the whole restaurant other than the one by the door that hasn't yet been laid. The lady is apologetic and courteous to a fault but they continue their ludicrous outburst, eventually asking to speak to the manager and generally behaving like spoilt children. Probably golfers. I make sure I leave a message at reception saying how wonderful I thought the service at breakfast was and how well the lady dealt with the moronic snobs. That's just the kind of selfless and gallant act you can expect from me, dear reader.

After donning the boots and backpack, I leave the hotel and head towards the road that will take me back to the path. I'm met by the very welcome sight of Pops and Tiny. They've made the long drive, early in the morning, to join me for one last hurrah on this epic trail. 'Blimey you look different' my Pops says as he eyes my leathery skin and loose-fitting clothes. It's so good to see the old boy and, as we fall into step together, I start to tell him about some of the recent sections, and the people and places I've come across since we last saw each other.

The walk begins with a ferry crossing to East Portlemouth. The only other passenger is a fellow walker, also with his sheepdog in tow. We soon get chatting and discover his name is Barry, and he's walking a seven day stretch of the path. As we chat, Tiny and Barry's dog do a stellar job of completely ignoring each other. Although, to be fair, Tiny is slightly pre-occupied with the concept of boat travel at this juncture. After the crossing, we part ways with them and continue along the woodland path, putting the world to rights as we do so. We pass a few elaborate waterside mansions, as the tree laden path crosses tracks and roads in a bid to leave civilisation behind.

Once we leave the woodland the trail picks up where it left off prior to Salcombe, and the scenery is staggeringly beautiful. This area is owned by the National Trust and as such does not disappoint. The thin undulating track winds up and down rocky outcrops and through the dramatic, unspoilt landscape. The skies are filled with a thickening mist that adds further atmosphere to the scene, as we hear the invisible waves crashing below us. Despite the mist, the air is still close with a sticky heat and, not for the first time, it's difficult to believe we're on the Devonshire coast rather than some far flung exotic location. Having recovered from the ferry crossing Tiny is revelling in the trek, as she runs off to explore her new surroundings and then periodically waits, impatiently, for us to catch up.

We pass the wonderfully named Gammon head and the secluded beauty of Elender Cove, before arriving at Prawle Point, where Pops has to turn back. We sit eating lunch, looking out to sea through the mist. We discuss some of the places I've still got ahead of me and how strange the idea of reaching the finishing line is. We say our goodbyes and I watch him disappear through the mist with Tiny by his side. A little emotional, I chomp down the final mouthful of the day's Mars Bar, apply the trusty stiff upper lip and venture forth once more.

The walking continues to be quintessential SWCP for the next few miles. Winding single file hillside tracks strewn with jagged rocks, above the crashing waves. The gulls, absent until now, appear above me; creating striking silhouettes amongst the mist, backlit by the obscured sun behind. I consult Rolly to discover I'm well over half way through the day's walk to the intriguingly named Beesands. Somewhere just before Start Point I catch up with Barry and his dog and we walk together for the remainder of the day.

Start Point is an impressive open space with majestic views in all directions. After swapping some walking stories, including the obligatory Hartland to Bude experience comparison, we exchange abridged life stories over the course of the next couple of hours. Barry is about 5,11' and probably the thinnest man currently alive. He looks like I imagine I would look if I just kept walking this path for the next twenty years without stopping. He has spent most of his life in the RAF and is now semi-retired, having to work part time in a supermarket to keep things comfortable. This seems a bit harsh for an ex-serviceman, all things considered, but then I've only just met the chap. Perhaps he's one of those peculiar people you hear about who enjoy working? To cut to the chase, Barry is a thoroughly good egg.

A few miles on and we arrive at the lost village of South Hallsands. A long since abandoned collection of cottages that have been half swallowed by the sea. The semi-ruins of houses that once made up a thriving fishing community, now edge ever closer to the merciless ocean. One by one they are claimed by the waves. The scene is made all the more gloriously spooky by the continued misty conditions. Barry explains that disaster originally struck when constructors, working on a nearby dockyard, basically pinched tons of shingle from underneath the ill-fated village. Although Rolly, not wishing to have his thunder stolen by the fancy pants real-life human new comer, quietly points out that this is, in fact, only rumour.

The remaining descent into Beesands is an easy one and once we arrive at the pub I've booked a room above, I say my goodbyes to Barry. He's off to nearby Torcross and I wish him all the very best for the rest of his trip. Beesands is a strange place, no two ways about it. A row of houses, including the pub I'm staying at, that are separated from the sea by a single-track road and a small concrete wall. It's completely flat and straight. It should, by all rights be an ugly place... but it isn't. It has a minimalist beauty to it that I'm struggling to convey. The pub is a decent gastro affair and my room a comforting back to basics number when compared to the luxury of the previous night. I call Pops and tell him about the rest of the walk. I then call up Tasha, my mum and speak to a few friends over WhatsApp. I order chips and a pint of ale and settle in for the evening.

The first few miles of the walk the following day are a surreal continuation of the flat straight line of Beesands. Through the village of Torcross and onto Slapton Ley. Torcross is Beesands but more so. Both villages and the subsequent section along Slapton Ley make for a very interesting change of terrain, unlike anything I've experienced thus far. That being said, after only a few miles, I'm glad they are an exception rather than a norm. I walk alongside the arrow straight, slightly elevated road, with a nature reserve on one side and the sea on the other. The mist and sticky heat of yesterday continue and are accompanied by frequent rain showers. Hundreds of gulls sit watching me as they bob up and down on the water.

The path does eventually rise up to the hilltops once I'm past Slapton, and get back to something approaching familiarity. I stride in and out of woodland sections and over sprawling farmland as the rain continues to intermittently fall. The mist eventually clears just in time for the impressive Blackpool sands to reveal itself through the tall imposing trees, that surround it. I emerge from the woodland to discover the yellow sands of this, usually full to bursting, picturesque beach nearly completely deserted. I decide there can be no better luncheon location and plonk myself down.

I delve into the backpack to pull out the last spicy sausage treat. I need to stock up when I arrive in Dartmouth later today and, in light of Mickey B's raised eyebrow, I've vowed to select a more ethically acceptable lunchtime treat for the remainder of the trip. I devour the sinful sausage in seconds. I cannot lie, I've come to relish the forbidden faux salami over the last few weeks. But, as some complete numpty once said, in some soul-destroying business seminar I once attended, in what now seems like another lifetime: be the change you want to see, people... I'm sorry dear reader, it was utterly unacceptable of me to subject you to a motivational mantra of such awfulness. Consider it fully retracted.

A short while later the path diverts inland around Stoke Fleming. The rain returns with force and I decide to seek shelter. I'm walking through a field next to a housing estate as the path heads back towards the sea. I duck into a shelter attached to some public toilets at the edge of the field, next to a small play park area. Within a couple of minutes, I'm joined by an older chap complete with walking poles, cagoule and backpack. It transpires that he's walking the whole of the Coast Path in the opposite direction to myself. We get chatting and, in a thick accent that I soon find out originates from Middlesbrough, he advises me that this is the second time he's walked the whole 630 miles.

'It gets to you, you'll see. You'll try other walks but this path never leaves you, you'll be back.' The first time he walked it he went the same way around as myself, and so I take the opportunity to ask what, on reflection, is a fool hardy question.

'Is the best of it behind me already?'

'Oh God yes, no doubt about that.' D'oh.

When the rain eventually eases up I wish him all the best and get going once more. As I approach the mouth of the River Dart I pass Dartmouth Castle; an impressive structure dating back to the 14th century. As the castle is now open to the public, the remaining path into Dartmouth itself is a well maintained and easy going wide track. It gently ambles through the wooded hillside overlooking the river, as I slowly descend into the attractive harbour town. I've arranged to meet Sophy and Dan for a second time in Dartmouth and then stay the night at theirs. Sophy is going to walk tomorrows stretch to Brixham with me, where we're then due to meet Tasha and Paddy.

Another pleasant evening ensues as we spend a few hours in a local pub, before heading back to theirs. At one point, we are accosted by an eccentric American woman in the pub garden. She is dressed as though it's the bleak mid-winter in Alaska, with a long trench coat, gloves and some kind of elaborate woolly hat. She decides to sit down next to us uninvited and share, in great detail, her garbled philosophy on life, the universe and everything. I mention this because my lasting memory of the event is our three individual reactions to our unwelcome guest, which, to my mind somehow capture our individual personalities perfectly. I shuffle uncomfortably and avoid eye contact, hoping that the whole embarrassing situation will just go away. Dan cheerily attempts to engage with the clearly heavily inebriated woman, in the belief that every stranger is just a friend you haven't met yet... no matter how strange the stranger. Sophy tells her she's an idiot and should probably get lost.

The Entourage Arrives, Agatha's House and Power Boat Racing on the English Riviera

Our walk begins across the water from Dartmouth, in Kingswear, the following morning. There is no sign of the mist from the last few days and the sunlit views down the river Dart are exceptional. Rolly, in the long-winded way I've become accustomed to in this troublesome third incarnation, tells me that the eleven-mile trek to Brixham is a tough one. The trickiest on the South Devon stretch in fact. It begins leisurely enough however as we amble along above the riverside, heading back towards the sea. We enjoy views of the castle standing majestically amongst the trees, before the path leads us into dense, tropical green woodland and then starts to climb.

I've always found it easy to talk to Sophy so it's a pleasure to have her company for the day's increasingly challenging walk. She expressed concern at joining me initially as it's been a while since she's done any decent length hiking. I have noticed with a few friends, come to think of it, that having a baby does have a tendency to dramatically cut into your fun time. In any event, she needn't have worried as we walk comfortably in step under the clear blue skies and warm sunshine. Having left the woodland behind the path is throwing up some mean climbs and drops as it winds through the increasingly rocky landscape.

We pass the twin points of Inner and Outer Frowland, with their second World War defence posts and views out to Mew Stone. Apparently Mew Stone (which is another way of saying Gull Rock, of which there are hundreds along the South West Coast Path) is prime seal spotting country. There's a fair few people about on this stretch, which would seem to lend credence to this notion. Alas, however, not a single one of the blighters about today. An awful lot of gulls though. I briefly entertain the idea that it's these brazen seabirds themselves that are spreading the rumour of seals around Mew Stone; with a view to enticing unsuspecting picnickers into their lair. If so it certainly seems to be working, as I watch them feigning an uninterested nonchalance, whilst creeping up on the numerous families munching on their sandwiches, blissfully unaware of the encroaching winged assassins.

The walking continues to be tough going in the run up to Scabbacombe Head. As the day wears on and we start to think about lunch, I take the opportunity to impart some hard-earned wisdom to my less experienced companion. 'The trick is Soph' I say, adopting an authoritative tone. 'To always stop for lunch at the top of a hill, never at the bottom of one.' She's looking impressed by this point. 'That way after you've rested and eaten you don't have a climb on a full stomach.' As we continue along the winding rocky path I'm sensing that Sophy, probably like Mickey B before her, is pretty overwhelmed by my zen-like relationship to my surroundings. I'm probably something akin to a spiritual guide to them. About 15 minutes or so later my blood sugar levels drop and, feeling a bit faint, I insist we stop for lunch immediately. At the bottom of a very steep hill. 'But I thought you were just saying…' 'Look Soph, it doesn't matter who said what. You really need to adopt a less structured approach if you're to survive life out here on the trail.'

After wolfing down our home-made sandwiches, we get going once more towards Scabbacombe sands, and then on to the superbly named Man Sands. Eventually we arrive, earlier than anticipated at the National Trust Café on Berry Head. The views out to the glimmering sea are fantastic and have been for most of the day. The sun is still beating down as we rest up with a couple of well-earned ice creams. There only remains an easy descent of a few miles down into Brixham harbour to meet Tasha and Paddy. Tasha calls me to let me know they have arrived and so, Mr Whippys duly dispensed with, we get moving again.

Brixham is a very attractive and bustling fishing town with a thriving tourist industry. It's built around the busy harbour, adorned with cafés, bars and restaurants. Tasha and Paddy are sat outside one such café, drinking tea and looking out over the water. We all greet each other enthusiastically and sit together for an hour or so, in the sunny picturesque spot. Soph heads off home but will return later with Dan and Ezra, to join us for dinner. Tasha, myself and Paddy are all staying in the same hotel and Paddy dutifully retires to his room, to allow us a couple of hours alone before we meet the others again.

Tasha tells me about the local council elections, where she did a sterling job, increasing the Greens share of the vote in her ward significantly. She also manages to assure me that Bovril is alive and definitely pining for me. His facial muscles are incapable of showing expression of any kind of course, but Tasha reassures me that she can clearly tell that he absolutely misses me, like the deserts miss the rain, no doubt about it. It's great to hear that all is well with the homestead. I regale with some of the highlights of the walk so far and we generally bask in each other's company for a while, before meeting up with Paddy again. Paddy, by way of introduction, is our next-door neighbour in Bristol. A dapper chap in his mid-eighties, who's always looked out for us and been only too happy to provide us with hot meals and plenty of booze over the years. He's a bit of a legend and it's really something that he's come all this way to see us. Although, knowing Paddy, he probably considered it his duty to accompany Tasha on the trip, to ensure a lady does not travel alone.

We meet up with Soph, Dan and Ezra and decide on one of the many fish and chip restaurants along the harbourside. We all enjoy the freshly caught delights on offer and a great evening is had by all. Outside the restaurant, we pose for a group photo and I realise, with a wry smile, that the entourage has finally arrived. If only the Big 630 man from Zennor could see me now. What's more we're meeting Mickey B and Hayley in the morning. But for now, I say my goodbyes to Soph, Dan and Ezra, for what will probably be the last time of the trip. I thank them for their kind hospitality, they wish me luck for the rest of the walk and we all promise to catch up again as soon as possible. Paddy then retires to bed and Tasha and I spend the remainder of the evening in a nearby pub, chatting with the odd local and watching the world go by.

We meet Mickey B and Hayley from the coach after breakfast the next morning, on what is already another glorious day. As, Mickey B notwithstanding, there is a general lack of enthusiasm regards joining me for a day's walking, (and taking into account that one of our party no longer has either of their original hips) I have planned a day out for us all. We are off to the National Trust owned Greenway's property, which was the summer residence of Agatha Christie and is now something of shrine to her. I'm a big Christie fan and my excitement at the day ahead is just enough to eclipse the fact that no other member of our jolly troupe as ever read anything by the esteemed queen of crime, or has any real interest in seeing where she summered. Fools.

Despite the lack of Agatha appreciation, the party is in tiptop spirits and the day out is a roaring success in the summer sunshine. The house itself is a large Georgian number set in acres of immaculate gardens. We wander round and listen to the engaging staff as they enthusiastically deliver a potted history of the residence, and its relationship to the great lady herself. We also take a walk down through the gardens, to the famous boathouse perched on the edge of the River Dart. Believed to be the actual boathouse from the classic novel Dead Man's Folly. We then take a well-earned rest at the on-site café, where we gorge on cake and banana milkshakes... or at least I do, I haven't really noticed what anyone else is gorging on... that's their business.

Later that afternoon, back in Brixham and it's time to say goodbye to Tasha and Paddy already. They've booked seats on a coach for the long trip back to Bristol and so we bid them adieu. I thank Paddy for making the effort to come all this way and he wishes me luck for the rest of the trip. Tasha and I say our farewells for the second time in six weeks and, as I kiss her goodbye and watch the coach pull away, I feel a strong pang of homesickness for the first time. Mickey B and Hayley are sticking around for an evening meal, and so the three of us head off in search of a restaurant along the harbour.

After dragging them both to a nearby launderette to give the old personals an overdue new leash of the good stuff, we settle for a large and bustling gastro pub overlooking the water for dinner. I bring Mickey B up to speed with how things have been going since I last saw him, and the ale and lime cordials are soon flowing freely. I also discuss with Hayley what action she intends to take, regards Mickey B's unforgivable behaviour, re the whole missing half a mile just outside Plymouth debacle. She advises me that this is the kind thing she has to put up with every day of her life. I sympathise with her. I mean to say dear reader; you meet someone, fall in love in good faith and then bang: twenty years later you realise you've ended up with a tee-total vegetarian from Barnsley, who is hell bent on sabotaging his friends best laid plans through sub-standard map reading.

As afternoon becomes evening I'm saying yet more goodbyes, as Mickey B and Hayley catch the bus out of town. After watching them go I wander back towards my hotel for the night and look over the pretty harbour in the fading light. I'm conscious that I'll now be alone for the remainder of this ever-evolving adventure. It feels like I've been walking forever, and yet at the same time like it's only just started and can't possibly be drawing to a close already. I focus on the immediate future and am comforted at the thought of adventures still yet to come. This incredible trail is not done with me just yet, and I am certainly not done with it.

I awake with a start and in a cold sweat the following morning, having had a terrible nightmare. I dreamt I was walking on the path next to the sea when I came across a large group of trendy hipster types drinking it; the sea that is. They were dipping large mugs and glasses into the ocean and then swigging it back. I could actually see the sea level dropping as they were doing this.

'Hey, what do you think you're doing?' I cry.

'We're drinking the sea' came the reply from one of their beardy number.

'But it's salted water?' I counter, quite reasonably I fancy.

'Of course, it's all the rage' one says with a growing distain at my ignorance, as those around him snigger and raise their eyebrows (threateningly) at me. 'We've had salted caramel and sea salt chocolate... now salted water is where it's at.' I stare incredulously as they continue to drain the ocean.

'Stop it' I scream, 'You're killing it... you're killing the sea you stupid, stupid hipsters.' They all look at me, unfazed by my outburst.

'Get a load of the square' one says. 'Hey square, why don't you buzz off... you square.' Then I look down and notice that

I'm sweating banana milkshake from every pour. I run. Well, what would you have done?

The short nine-mile walk to Torquay begins with a decent stroll through the woods. It feels great to be back on the trail again and I have to check my excitement, as at my current speed I'll arrive in Torquay before lunch. It's another clear and sunny day and I'm even braving the shorts. My head and arms, as previously mentioned, are tanned brown to a leathery degree. The old legs on the other hand, having hardly seen the light of day, are by contrast a brilliant white. The overall effect is that I'm wearing somebody else's legs. As I emerge from the woods I begin to pass picturesque beaches, including the pretty and secluded Elbery Cove. Here I decide a paddle is in order, and spend a satisfying twenty minutes or so splashing around contentedly, like an elderly Labrador might do.

After one or two reasonable climbs, I walk alongside a railway line for a brief stretch in the approach to Paignton. Following a small inland diversion, I pass under an impressive viaduct before reaching Godrington sands. The long rows of beach huts here, with their immaculately painted front doors in every imaginable colour evoke a, somehow nostalgic, reaction in me. As though they are transporting me back to childhood, but not my own. Conjuring up so many quintessentially British seaside images from postcards and paintings of times gone by. The circling and swooping gulls overhead completing the picture.

The walking is now flat and easy and if I'm honest, a touch uninspiring. More beach huts follow not long after at Corbyn beach. They are soon accompanied by more latter twentieth century human detritus, in the form of arcades and waterslides. I feel as though I'm taking a tour of the British seaside through the ages. Passing from the quaint beach huts and stripy deck chairs of times gone by into the, now slightly dilapidated, neon arcades and hot dog stands of my own youth. Dilapidated they may be, but the enticing beach front establishments are enjoying a roaring trade in today's clement conditions.

As I approach Torquay and the panoramic views of the city emerge through the haze in front of me, I'm struck initially by how attractive it all looks. I've never been to Torquay and, based largely on Fawlty Towers, as well as hearing various derogatory japes at its expense regarding its moniker as the English Riviera, I was expecting a bit of a dump. I'm a big fan of us Brits tendency towards self-deprecation, but I do think we sometimes do down our green and pleasant land unjustly. The view in front of me now, for example, would rival many a plush European coastal city. Stylish architecture, swanky hotels and a bustling attractive harbourside, glimmer and sparkle in the bright sunshine. All sat atop cliffs of a deep red colour, rising from the calm blue ocean below.

After a pleasant wander around the pier I find a spot to sit and eat lunch. Crowds are gathering nearby and the reason why soon becomes apparent. The roar of engines can be heard out to sea and a loud voice booms suddenly from a loud speaker situated above my head... a fact I was unaware of until this exact moment. Apparently, there is an afternoon of powerboat racing in store. Fair enough. I sit and watch for the next hour or so as the vessels zoom around at breakneck speeds and jostle for position, to the whoops and cheers of the crowds. It's all good fun and I'm in good spirits as I wander off towards my hotel for the evening. A slightly run down, out of town establishment with pink fluffy carpets and avocado bathroom furniture. Perfectly pleasant however and I spend a relaxing evening pottering around and writing up some notes.

Post breakfasting on the much aforementioned wheat biscuit delights the following morning, it seems to be taking me an age to leave Torquay behind. I'm still in a distinctly residential area as I pass a striking solitary offshore rock known as Hope's Nose. Once I do finally leave the urban sprawl however, the path becomes surprisingly attractive in the run up to Babbacombe. In particular the dramatically jagged Anstey's Cove with its prominent and sharply pointed rock formations, jutting out to sea. Despite the rawness of the landscape I'm still very much in an inhabited area; the path itself is flat and manicured and the odd passing yacht or fancy pants sailboat, lets me know I'm still in range of Torquay.

Fortunately, once I pass the beaches of Babbacombe, the views stretching out ahead of me are wild and staggeringly beautiful. Luscious tropical green treetops adorn the rich red sandstone cliffs for miles ahead. The deep blue sea turns blood red as it mixes with the soil by the shoreline. The path itself climbs and falls steeply and I'm revelling in the challenge of it as I pass repeatedly between deep dark woodlands and open rolling green farmland. Herds of dozing cattle relax in the dry heat as I stride past purposefully. As scores of vocal gulls and crows squabble in the skies above me, I'm back where I should be; where I need to be. A solitary moving dot on a vast ancient landscape. The path, the sea and me. Forever onwards.

As I pass through Maidencombe I consult Rolly, who advises me that this area is home to a rare species of bird called the Cirl Bunting. Chubby little critters the size of a Sparrow with yellow and brown markings. They've been re-introduced to the area by the RSPB and thanks to their efforts, can now be seen relatively frequently. I spy a few along the next mile or so and realise that I've seen them before, at various points over the last few days. I think of all the different species of hedgerow birds I've encountered along this journey. Mile after mile they've provided so much of the soundtrack to the walk so far. I'm annoyed with myself for making no effort whatsoever to learn the names of the many varieties I've seen, and vow to put this right in the future.

The decent walking continues as I pass Labrador Bay and beyond. Having said that, some of the woodland sections stretch on for long enough that find myself missing the sea for increasing periods of time throughout the day. The sound of the waves remains audible through the dark dense bushes and trees but miles seem to go by without even a glimpse. This does eventually change however and with a reassuringly tree free view in front of me I stop for a late lunch.

I have a confession to make dear reader. I've been avoiding telling you these last few days. I've purchased more processed spicy sausage snacks. Listen, I have a problem OK? I need sympathy and support, not judgement. I went into the shop in Brixham with the very best of intentions, honestly I did. But what can I do? Cheese is out... we've learnt that. I'm smelly and sweaty enough as it is without re-introducing more smelliness and... um, sweatiness. Sandwiches of any description aren't going to last days on end in my backpack; so, you see, my hands are tied. I'm not proud... even though they do taste ruddy yummy. I'll become a vegan when I finish the walk or something. Or only eat roadkill maybe. Anyway, I scoff down the forbidden meaty snack and move on to the trusty Mars Bar. When this book becomes an international best seller the good people of the Mars corporation will probably send me a free life time supply of Mars Bars, on account of the free positive advertising. I should make it clear therefore, that I will also accept Mars ice creams or Mars milkshakes. But don't try and fob me off with Snickers, I'm not Mr T.

The afternoon jaunt toward my final destination of Teignmouth is highly enjoyable in the summery conditions. The path leads me through further open farmland, with decent ups and downs and a continued backdrop of far reaching views in each direction. Eventually I arrive at the mouth of the river Teign, where I must catch the foot ferry to the other side. An impromptu meet up with an old friend awaits me in Teignmouth. I was convinced I'd seen the last of the visitors on this trip and so it's come as a pleasant surprise.

Lou is a lovely lady I used to work with and who lives in nearby Newton Abbott. She's very kindly arranged to pop over and treat me to a pint in Teignmouth. I meet her on the promenade and we head into town and to the nearest pub. She brings her huge, gangly and loveable dog Bodie along. I remember countless teleconferences through work where the sound of Bodie barking in the background put many a speaker off their stride, so it's a pleasure to be able to put a face to the bark at last. We sit out in the afternoon sun supping beer and eating chips. I re-tell some, by now, tried and tested anecdotes from the trip so far and we generally gossip like a pair of old codgers. After a couple of hours, we say our goodbyes and I head off toward my hotel for the night.

I've been using an app on my phone to book the pubs, hotels, B&B's and campsites that I've frequented throughout the journey so far. Usually picking the cheapest one and booking it up the night before, or morning of, my expected arrival. Generally, this has gone pretty smoothly with no real surprises. Tonight, however I have inadvertently booked into a hotel for the visually impaired. I know this to be the case even before I enter the building due, for the most part, to the large signs clearly stating that this is a hotel for the visually impaired. I'm slightly nervous as I approach the main entrance as I'm not sure if it's a hotel *exclusively* for the visually impaired. The lady at reception does look at me a touch suspiciously but, to be fair this could be for any number of reasons, and ultimately the transaction unfolds with no issues. For fairly obvious reasons, I've never been inside a building built specially for the visually impaired before and I'm amazed by the ingenuity of the place. All the floors are sloped at certain angles and the corridors are of varying widths to allow the clientele to navigate their way around freely. I keep nearly tripping over as I try to acclimatise to this.

Later that evening I wander back to the pub and spend some time working on my album of walking themed classics, concerned that I may have been neglecting it of late. I come up with: 'Do you know the way to Booby's Bay?' (You know, as in 'do you know the way to San Jose?') I practically write the whole thing: 'Do you know the way to Booby's Bay? I've got to find some peace of mind in Booby's Bay. Plymouth is a great big feeling, it can leave you far away from home. With a dream in your heart you're never alone. But dreams turn into dust and fly away, and there you are, without a prayer, you're walking tracks and lugging packs.' I assume I don't need to waste any time conveying to you how pleased I am with this masterpiece.

The Red Seas, The Mighty Jungle and Something to do with Jane Austen?

I begin the next day by popping a giant blister on my big toe and then eating four Weetabix. I'm a man of extremes. For today's walk I've elected to stroll a meagre seven-and-a-half-miles and stopover in nearby Exmouth. This recent bout of short walks is fooling nobody I realise, least of all myself. It's doubtless clear to one and all that I'm attempting to drag out the remainder of the trail and savour every last step between here and Poole. As I leave the hotel the skies are filled with thick dark clouds, and a stiff wind ensures a noticeably colder temperature than of late.

The gulls are out in force this morning and I watch them squabbling, washing themselves amongst the waves and gliding gracefully overhead, as I take the easy walk along the promenade out of Teignmouth. Even though the walking remains flat all the way to Holcombe, I'm enjoying being so close to the sea after seeing so little of it for long periods through the dense woodlands yesterday. The distant horizon where the endless blanket of silky water meets the sky is as mesmerising and mysterious to me now as it was leaving Minehead on day one. A few small ascents and descents through Holcombe fail to provide any physical challenge, but do reveal further impressive examples of the distinctive red cliffs that have characterised the coastline since Torquay.

Somewhere around Dawlish the path beings to run adjacent to a railway line. As with a previous stretch close to Penzance the path is all that separates the sea on one side from the train track on the other. The effect is even more startling on this occasion however, as both the railway line and sea are that much closer to the thin concrete walkway. The path is only accessible at low tide and its pure luck that I'm able to experience it as, and this may shock you dear reader, I've not learnt my lesson re checking the tide times. Wading through water armpit deep and costly enforced taxi rides are, apparently, not severe enough inconveniences to stir me into the complex action of taking two full minutes to check my phone each evening.

Some tedious inland walking ensues thereafter as I'm diverted away from the coast. This includes passing through a, seemingly endless, caravan and holiday park complex that brings with it the sudden emergence of crowds of people dressed for the beach. The rain has thus far held off but the clouds still loom overhead and the wind still brings with it a distinct chill. It's a scene that makes you proud to be British; as scores of determined holiday makers stream past in shorts and flip flops whilst their shivering children desperately clasp buckets and spades with a steely resolve. As the path winds its way back towards the sea I pass through residential areas in need of some regeneration, and am pleased when Starcross railway station finally appears ahead.

Rolly advises me that the ferry crossing to Exmouth departs from somewhere next to the tiny open-air station, and so I wander through in search of the pick-up point. I have an hour to wait before the first ferry and it's not even lunch time. I make a decision there and then that there'll be no more short walks to prolong reaching the finish line. It's a false economy as I'm only getting half a day's walking in and there's too much hanging around involved. On the plus side, the wait at the ferry port yields another song idea. As I sit staring out across the River Exe inspiration strikes and I come up with: 'Let's talk about Exe, baby.' You know like the Salt 'n' Pepa classic? I know, I know: Brilliant, right?

When the larger-than-I'm-used-to passenger ferry arrives I'm still the only one waiting. I climb on board, take a seat and sling my backpack onto the floor in front of me, humming 'let's talk about Exe' all the while. Just before the boat is due to depart a couple climb on board and sit in the seats next to mine. A giant of a man with hands the size of gammon steaks and a smiley faced blonde woman, with matching blue puffa jackets.

'Good Lord what happened to you lad?' says the giant, looking directly at me.

'Err… what do you mean?' I reply, suddenly feeling self-conscious.

He turns to look at his partner; 'Have we got any change to give this young lad pet? He's down on his luck.' There's a brief silence, during which my brain tries in vain to process a mountain of conflicting emotions, including embarrassment, hurt, shock and confusion. But then he bursts out laughing, as his partner rolls her eyes in mock exasperation. 'I'm only messing with you lad.' He gives me a playful punch on the shoulder, which actually really hurts. 'You must be walking the Coast Path?' I regain my composure.

'Oh… err… yes that's right.'

The three of us chat through the rest of the journey and I find it impossible not to warm to their infectious personalities.

'Where did you start?' The woman asks.

'Minehead, can't believe it's nearly over already.'

They bolster my ego with some words of congratulations.

'You know, I've always thought I'd like to walk that walk one day' says the friendly giant. His partner laughs and affectionately pats his pot belly.

'That'll be the day pet, that'll be the day.'

'I reckon I was a stone and a half heavier when I started' I chip in.

'Really?' she replies, turning back to her partner enthusiastically.

'Well maybe you should walk it twice then lover.'

After arriving in Exmouth and saying my goodbyes to my sailing companions, I find my hotel and check in for the evening. Past its prime doesn't really cover this one, dear reader. My room is a postage stamp that clearly hasn't had another human in it since the mid-seventies. The door only opens a crack because the bed fills the entire room. The en-suite is a small wardrobe in the corner and I have to climb on the toilet to close the door, so I can then access the shower. The décor is a fetching faded violet and mauve ensemble and there's an unidentified layer of stickiness covering everything from floor to ceiling. Still, all good fun. It's dirt cheap and by the seaside after all.

By the time I sit down to breakfast the following morning my chipper acceptance of my jaded lodgings is in danger of wearing thin. I'm sitting at a small sticky table, on a wobbly sticky chair, in a cold dark dining room. I'm watching as rows of ants appear from my salt and pepper dispensers and attempt to make the arduous journey across the table top. It's too sticky for most of them and they are left stranded in the invisible goo, in danger of losing limbs. A few of the hardier souls reach the safety of my cutlery and set up camp, surveying the carnage of the battle field behind them. I'm moved to try and help some of the little blighters on their way, but I'm not all that keen on touching anything else inside the hotel from this point on. With the exception of the front door handle, and this is only through absolute necessity.

Exmouth, like so many of the fading seaside towns along the south coast, gives the distinct impression that it fully expects it to be raining when you arrive. That being said, as I stroll along the esplanade towards the enticing cliffs in the far distance, I must concede that it makes a better fist of it than most. Away from the main strip, the attractive stone wall that separates the sea from the path is adorned with Victorian street lamps and the yellow sands that run down to the sea do at least tip their hat to the notion of a sunny day. The weather this morning however is a continuation of the dark, moody skies and blustery winds of the previous day.

After a mile or so I reach the end of the esplanade and arrive at an area called Orcombe Red Rocks. A sign proudly proclaims that this is the oldest section of the Jurassic Coast World Heritage Site. I climb the zig zag path to the clifftop where a grassy track leads to the Geoneedle at Orcombe Point. An impressive structure built using stone and rock found on the Jurassic coast. The views really open up here as well and the scene in front of me has a distinct Jurassic feel to it. Vast red cliffs, sporadically adorned with rich dark green flora, sloping down into the frothing red seas below. I half expect to see a Pterodactyl glide by. The views in the other direction back to Exmouth and beyond are almost as equally striking and I have a mounting optimism about the day ahead. Rolly seems a bit a lukewarm in this regard however. Although, I haven't got to know him in his latest guise as yet. That's right dear reader, the troublesome Rolly 3 has shuffled off this mortal coil. A sticky violet and mauve box room in Exmouth is his final resting place. Rolly 4 has arrived. The final Rolly. The last guidebook to see me home.

After a short but exhilarating stretch of clifftop walking with continued views in either direction, Rolly's tepid attitude towards the walk ahead is fully justified. The double whammy of an army rifle range on one side and a gigantic caravan park on the other comes into view. I begrudgingly navigate my way through the seemingly never-ending rows of mobile homes, distinguishable only by the signs above the doors. Names like 'The Cedars', 'The Bordeaux' and 'The Windrush.' Anything as long as it's pre-fixed with 'the.' It seems to take an age to reach the other side but when I do the sight in front of me is a pleasing one. I can see the village of Budleigh Salterton, where I intend to stop for lunch, in the distance. Between me and it stands what looks like a decent stretch of challenging cliff edge walking.

This turns out to be half true. The next mile or so involves a decent climb and some more beautiful scenery. The descent towards Budleigh on the other hand yields a golf course, some manicured pathways and a sudden down pouring of rain. When I do arrive in the village though, the sun is shining and I quickly dry off as I stroll along the seafront. It strikes me that if I'd have walked a proper distance yesterday I could have stayed in Budleigh Salterton rather than Exmouth. It's an attractive spot, with rows of colourfully painted fishing boats and old-fashioned beach huts lined up along the picturesque pebbly beach. I pass a sign that proclaims it an unspoilt village set amongst an area of outstanding natural beauty. I think about the notion of an 'unspoilt' village and what that description is actually telling me. 'Look everyone we've found a bit that we as a species haven't completely ruined yet! Quick everyone, gather here.' I think of all the 'spoilt' locations I've passed through in the last few weeks.

The beach front path eventually gives way to the promisingly named Otter Estuary Nature Reserve. I don't see any otters unfortunately, but the inland stretch through the reserve and out to the cliffs on the other side is a pleasant enough one. A flat path navigating around the River Otter through attractive tall trees, salt marshes and a variety of contented birdlife. Once I'm on the other side I find a bench and stop for lunch. Mid-chomp I hear a strange noise that sounds a bit like a cat's meow. I turn to see a gull staring up at me. It meows again. I wonder if the strange and distinctly un-gull like noise signifies that it's injured in some way. I offer it some food, which it hoovers up immediately before turning to face me again and emitting the meow once more. It takes the sacrifice of a few more bites of my lunch before I realise what's really happening here. Blessed with this unique defect of birth, the bird has masterfully turned it round to its advantage. As I note how rotund the creature is, it's suddenly all too clear that I've fallen for a well-rehearsed act. Cunning little blighter.

The afternoon's walk returns to the clifftops as the weather continues to improve. A patchwork of rolling farmland stretches off to my left, but I'm spending most of my time looking out across the sea. It's staggeringly beautiful along this section. A seductive silky, pearly blanket of water that emits a heavenly glow from underneath the dramatic low cover of vibrant clouds. The cliffs bleeding their red soil in from directly beneath me, complete the other worldly feel of my surroundings. The views in front of me spread out into the distance and I get my first sight of the path beyond the red cliffs. Vast stretches of iconic chalk white coastline tantalisingly begin to emerge up ahead.

I pass through Ladram Bay and another holiday park. This is a smaller affair though and I barely notice it as I continue to gaze out across the water. Huge detached clumps of sandstone cliff protrude from the lapping waves offshore, circled by skilfully swooping seabirds. I continue to stare open mouthed in awe, privileged to be witnessing the daily dramas of a 250-

million-year-old landscape play out before me. I enter a stretch of woodland that will lead me down into my final destination for the day; the upmarket seaside resort of Sidmouth.

After checking into my hotel, a vast improvement on the previous nights, I head straight back out to continue gazing at the pearly ocean. I spend the evening like this, finding a pub on the seafront with outdoor seating facing out to sea. I call the loved ones and relay back to them the day's trek. A mixed bag of a walk. Some truly spectacular (if all too short) stretches, interrupted by flat uninspiring and inhabited sections. As ever with this trail though, the stunning views bring with them the promise of the future. The eternal tomorrow.

Early the following morning I'm climbing up through a beautiful stretch of woodland covered in a blanket of bluebells. The delicate prettiness of the scene is in direct contrast to the severity of the climb. The pack is weighing heavy but I'm grinning through the sweat as I reach the clifftop and am met by the first views of the day. Rolly has forewarned me regards the severity of today's hike to the fantastically and thirst quenchingly named village of Beer. I realise that I'm not just prepared for the tough trek but am revelling in the prospect of it. It's difficult to pin point exactly when this change of attitude took place, perhaps it's been a gradual realisation. Whatever the truth, at some point over the last 530 miles, I went from fearing the tough climbs to craving them.

Over the next few miles the path sets about testing this new found cavalier attitude by throwing everything it has at me. Gloriously vicious ascents and drops follow each other in quick succession as I pass Salcombe Mouth, and head towards Weston Mouth. This section is hands down the best stretch of walking I've experienced in what suddenly feels like ages. Up until now if I was to compose a list of top ten walks of the trail so far there would be a strong chance that they'd all be from the north coast, prior to Lands' End. Every step I'm taking currently is further confirmation that this is no longer the case. The path winds itself aggressively along the edge of the dramatic landscape. I pass the stunning Lyme Cove where it looks as though the sea has reached out and torn great chunks of the land away.

The climbs continue to come thick and fast. At the peak of a particularly tough ascent I pause to catch my breath. I survey the vast landscape below me. Through a clump trees I see a group of deer running free. A buzzard, the first I've seen in... again what suddenly seems like an age, appears and hovers majestically. The bird is at my head height across the other side of the cove as I watch it circle, completely immersed. I feel momentarily overcome by a wave of emotion at what I'm looking at. This feeling of wilderness is one that's been sorely missing in recent days. I continue on my way, passing more wildlife as a group of horses cross the path ahead of me, emerging from over the hillside.

I stop for lunch in Branscombe before passing through more picturesque woodlands. A few miles later I reach the first of the white cliffs that have been part of the view for the last day or so. As I approach Beer Head the scene is as wondrous as the path is challenging. The rich red giving way to the chalky white as the ups and downs continue. I reach a beautiful area called the Hooken Cliffs. This brings me to a stretch named Under Hooken, which takes me beneath the huge imposing cliffs and along an undulating track, passing through the undergrowth. To see the cliffs from this new vantage point, looking up at their imposing stature, is simply fantastic. The section ends with a steep climb back up to the clifftop.

From there I begin the long descent into Beer. The village has an instantly more welcoming feel to it than anywhere I've been in the last few days. A pretty cove that feels wonderfully sleepy, despite the crowded beer garden and deck chair strewn beach front. I pass a plot of allotments on the way in and can't think of a better spot to grow your marrows from. The shimmering sea gently laps at the sand in the afternoon sunshine as I make my way toward my bed for the night. The Dolphin Inn turns out to be one of my favourite pubs and hotels along the whole Coast Path. A friendly welcome, affordable and comfortable rooms and a decent, laid back bar and restaurant.

Later that evening I dine on scallops and potatoes (not chips), chat to the bar staff for a while and write up a few notes. I then head back out towards the sea to join the crowds in the beer garden that overlooks the beachfront. As I sit I look across at the path that leads steeply up the side of the cliff and out of the village, for the start of tomorrows walk. Here I remain, sipping contentedly as evening slowly changes to night and the velvety ocean fades into darkness. The perfect end to a perfect day.

The walk to Lyme Regis the following morning, after a steep climb, begins with a trek into the village of Seaton. Rolly gets very excited as I pass over Axmouth bridge and is keen to convey to me it's historical importance. I'm afraid I'm only half listening though, as I'm too busy hoping that the uninspiring pavement walking soon turns into something akin to the wilderness of yesterday. Things aren't looking promising as I'm met with the unwelcome sight of yet another golf course around Axe Cliff. A short spell along an overgrown country track follows thereafter. The sun is out and in full swing now and I'm getting a definite summer stroll vibe, as flowers adorn the hedgerows on either side of the track. Then I come across a sign.

I've reached the start of Undercliff National Nature Reserve and the sign is a warning of what lays ahead. A six-mile stretch deep in the dense wild woodland with no alternate escape routes until you reach the other side. Rolly had advised this was coming but, in the excitement of yesterday, I'd forgotten all about it. It's a stretch I've been looking forward to and my spirits soar as I take the thin path leading down into the rich vegetation. The path is slippery with mud as it winds downwards and the sky disappears above me. I'm struck by an almost instant humidity in the air as I go deeper. The whole thing feels like I've just wandered into the jungle. I mean I've never actually been to the jungle, but you get the general gist of things I'm sure.

What follows does not disappoint. The path winds through its thick lush green surroundings as the terrain becomes gradually tougher. At times I'm climbing over fallen trees and splashing through muddy bogs. I see occasional glimpses of the sea on one side and huge white cliffs on the other. The humidity continues to intensify and I'm sweating buckets, as I clamber through the bushes. The wildlife is out in abundance too and I'm constantly batting away all manner of creepy crawlies, as a chorus of birdsong rings out. At one point, I see a pair of shiny eyes staring at me through the vegetation. A fox watching-me-pass-by turns and runs when I make eye contact. Over the next few miles I see dragon flies, butterflies, many different species of bird and even a deer or two. Around each corner is something new and unexpected as the path continues to navigate its way through the undergrowth. The views around Whitlands Cliff in particular are immense and a reminder that what you are walking through is, in effect, a vast landslip.

When I do eventually emerge from the jungle, I climb out into open fields with far reaching views. The contrast is startling and I need a few minutes to get used to the bright sunshine. There are views to Lyme Regis in front of me as I walk onwards and the sight of the calm endless sea warms my bones. At some point over the next mile or so I pass the county border into Dorset. Devon - like Cornwall - is now a thing of the past. Dorset is the final county (Da de da da, da de da da da). You know, as in the Final Countdown... by eighties rockers Europe? That one's going on the LP for sure. I continue across the fields, past a small stream and down one last steep wooded descent, before emerging at the harbourside of this popular tourist spot.

The first thing anyone arriving in Lyme Regis will notice is the famous Cobb. The harbour construction dating back to medieval times. It's of huge historical importance, playing significant roles in the sinking of the Spanish Armada and in the defeat of the Royalists during the English civil war. It's also got something to do with Jane Austen, apparently. I stroll along it and then onto the beach, soaking up the atmosphere of the bustling seafront before heading inland to find the pub I'm staying in.

All in all, it's not a bad start for Dorset; Lyme Regis is a pretty, if over-priced, place with a few nice-looking pubs and places to eat. After checking in I wander back down and decide on a Pizza restaurant for dinner. Whilst quaffing down a quattro formaggi I think back on the last two days of walking. What a spectacular and fitting way for Devon to sign off from the trail.

5. Dorset

The Wrong Pub, Portland Bill and The Final County
(Da de da da, da de da da da)

The following day begins with a long and arduous inland diversion between Lyme Regis and Charmouth. The whole of this section of path is closed due to erosion, and the diverted route follows a busy and unpleasant main road the entire way. The majority of the time there is no pavement and there are more than a few hairy moments. The situation isn't helped by the weather. A thick fog is accompanied by a driving wind and intermittent down pours. So bad is the situation that by the time I reach the golf course near Langmoor Manor, I'm actually pleased to see it. The weather ensures that even the most committed of the argyle brigade has stayed at home, and so the trudge across the green is a welcome respite. It doesn't last however and the path soon spits me back out onto the road once more. The long walk from there down to the front at Charmouth is a cold, wet and insanely perilous one. It then gets slightly better for the next few miles in the run up to Stonebarrow, as I walk along a country lane, still nowhere near the sea.

From there I finally pick up the Coast Path proper again and head towards Golden Cap, which Rolly advises me is the highest point of the south coast of England. The fog is still thickening and I can barely see my feet below me, let alone the cliff edge. The rain is now constant and the driving wind all the more intense now I'm back on the coast. The path itself is climbing and falling steeply and, in other circumstances, I get the impression this may be an exhilarating section. Here and now however, I'm struggling. My mood is dark following my dice with death along the busy roads earlier, and the conditions are now in the realms of the genuinely treacherous. Any notion of the views that normally accompany a high peak on this trail are foolhardy, as I clamber blindly onwards through fog and wind.

By the time I make it to the tiny village of Seatown I'm exhausted and soaked to the bone. I make an executive decision and head to the local pub for lunch. This proves to be the first decent move of the day. It would be hasty to claim I reach anything approaching dryness, but I certainly warm up a good deal in front of the fire place in the tiny front room. I stay there nursing a pint for over an hour in the hope that the weather will ease. It doesn't however and with an eye on the time I come to the realisation that I need to get back out there. I prolong the inevitable a little while longer by purchasing a second bag of pickled onion crisps. To the incredulous stares of the bar staff and clientele, I then put back on my soaking wet coat, sling the pack on my back and brave the storm. What a guy.

The afternoon's walk is more of the same as the rain and wind actually get worse. The fog loses a bit of its intensity somewhere around Throncombe Beacon. Although not enough to actually see anything of what Rolly advises are magnificent views. A long and relatively gentle descent follows in the run up to Eype Mouth. Here I must negotiate slippery stepping stones to get over the water, before a steep climb back up the cliff again. The remaining few miles to West Bay stay along the clifftop and as the fog continues to clear I begin to get the first proper views of the day. The cliffs have again changed colour; from the chalky white of the last few days to a striking yellow sandstone. As I approach West Bay I keep my eyes open for waymarkers for another trail; the Monarch's Way. I was unable to find anywhere to stay in West Bay and so need to walk an extra few miles inland to the nearby town of Bridport, where I've booked a room above a pub.

By the time I arrive in the small and attractive town centre the rain has finally stopped and the wind died down. My spirits are beginning to rise as I pass a number of appetising restaurants and swanky bistro pubs. I then spy mine. I stand looking at it from the across the street. I double check my reservation. I even google it to make sure there aren't two pubs in Bridport with the same name. There aren't. Every window is covered by a St George flag and a skin-headed man in turned up jeans and tightly laced Dr Martins stands outside the front door smoking. Looking like a drowned rat, I reluctantly approach and enter into the bar. Heads turn in my direction and there's a brief movie-western-style silence before the shaven headed clientele return to their pints. I'm shown to my room by a woman visibly weighed down with gold rings, earrings and enough necklaces to put Mr T to shame. The 'en-suite' bathroom, which is three doors down along the hall, doesn't have a lock so I'm advised to knock before entering.

I do my best to get dried off before leaving the pub with no intention of returning until I need to sleep. I spend the evening in a decent nearby pub and return to my room at about eleven at night. I return to find a full-scale party underway, complete with wall-to-wall sound system. My room is directly above and is - literally - shaking with the sound of the bass. I sit awake for the next three hours until the music finally stops. During that time, there are at least two proper fights outside my window and a couple of mere skirmishes. Now, I'm conscious of sounding like a snob here. I hope I'm someone that endeavours not to judge a book by its cover in this life. However, do you know what I've learnt in the last six hours? That sometimes, dear reader, you can judge a book by its cover. Every now and then a person or a place is *exactly* what it or they first appear to be.

Unsurprisingly I don't sleep a wink for the remainder of the night. Being a naturally optimistic chap however, I do use the time wisely. Partly thinking about, somewhat ironically given the current circumstances, how this trip has (fingers crossed) rid me of my insomnia. I had, as previously mentioned, already discovered the extraordinary benefits of walking long distances in that regard. Nevertheless, I was fully expecting a good many more restless nights on this trip. Hours spent conversing with my disobedient conscience, attempting to coax the blighter into sleep. As it stands my conscience and I have, barring the odd spat, got on like a house on fire thus far. I've even grown rather fond of the old chap.

Back on point however, I also use the time to book accommodation for the next few nights via the app on my phone. In light of recent events I take a good deal more interest in this than usual; reading countless reviews of each pub or hotel, instead of just finding the cheapest option. In addition to this I listen to an entire Wodehouse audiobook. It simply isn't possible to remain glum when reading Wodehouse. Lastly, I sit looking out of the window waiting for the first cracks of daylight. When they arrive I leave the premises at lightning speed, posting my room and front door keys back through the letterbox as I march off toward the sea.

The walk back to West Bay is one without particular merit, but I enjoy it immensely as every step takes me closer to the ocean and further from Bridport. When I arrive my first task is to climb the steep hillside to the top of the impressive East Cliffs. At the time of my arrival the area is enjoying notoriety thanks to the popular TV show; Broadchurch, which uses the vast sandstone cliff as it's backdrop. A short stretch of clifftop walking follows where I ignore the golf course to my left and gaze lovingly out to sea. It's a warm summers day and I feel the trials and tribulations of the previous 24 hours evaporate across the sparkling water. A pair of gulls appear from below the cliff edge and fly beside me at head height for a few hundred yards, as if welcoming me back on to the trail and ensuring I'm still in one piece.

I descend into Burton Bradstock, where Rolly advises me I must walk inland along the river for a short while, before climbing the next steep hill to the summit of Burton Cliff. A brief diversion follows due to coastal erosion before another enjoyable spell along the cliff edge. I realise I'm repeating another senseless mantra as I stride onwards. Another random snippet of internal monologue that has escaped from my subconscious, and become stuck in my throat. 'Stephen Fry is a very nice guy; Stephen Fry is a very nice guy.' I wonder how long I've been saying this out loud as I concentrate on breaking the maddening loop. After a while the path drops down onto Cogden beach and the far-reaching views ahead of me convey that a long flat stretch of walking will form the remainder of the day's hike to Abbotsbury.

Along the way there are few long and cumbersome sections that involve traipsing across loose pebbles for miles on end. With boots and a heavy backpack this is increasingly unpleasant work. As I slowly and comically plod through endless mountains of the remorseless tiny rocks, I realise that I probably look very similar to a man that's just rubbed an entire tube of expired ibuprofen gel on his feet, or Mr Soft from the Softmints adverts. After a while I converse with Rolly to discover that Cogden Beach is part of the famous pebble ridge called Chesil Bank, which leads all the way to Weymouth. A wave of nausea washes over me as I contemplate the prospect of two full days walking on pebbles. So far Dorset has given me two decent cliffs and a whole lot of misery.

My anti Dorset stance was thankfully premature however, as the landscape changes shortly thereafter. I soon find myself walking along a track behind the beach for a few miles, where I resume my enjoyment of the hot and sunny day. The cloudless

143

blue sky to my right is inhabited by noisy gulls and crows vying for air space, whilst in the distance to my left I spy a hovering bird of prey across the patchwork fields. Stretching out in front of me are views of Portland Island, with its famous lighthouse silhouetted against the horizon. The landscape between here and Portland is visually striking, as the flat green fields wind in and out against the strip of water that separates them from Chesil Bank and then the mighty ocean beyond.

The path then curves inland away from the sea as it heads for Abbotsbury. The first thing I notice is the arresting sight of the Chapel of St Catherine's, stood alone atop the hill in front of me. I climb up to it on my way into the village and have a good old nose around the ancient structure. It's far smaller than its prime vantage point on the hill at first makes it appear, but is nonetheless impressive for it. After soaking up the views for a few minutes I wander down into Abbotsbury itself. The beautiful country village with its popular Swannery and picture postcard high street is a welcome sight indeed. The pretty upmarket pub that I'm booked into for the night provides the perfect antidote to the previous nights' lodgings. I spend a relaxing evening in the pub garden before retiring to my room for a long and peaceful nights' sleep.

Feeling refreshed and full to the brim with a sense of plucky thingamy-bobs, I leave early the next morning to begin the 13-mile trek to Weymouth. The path ambles its way through attractive farmland full of playful lambs and their sleep deprived mothers, dozing in the bright Dorset sunshine. I stroll contentedly down a few country lanes, passing the Swannery and off into the English countryside. One or two steep climbs and drops ensue followed by a stretch along a hillside ridge, all the while remaining a few miles inland. Sometime later the path finally turns right and begins to head towards the sea. I walk steeply downhill for good while, through flourishing arable fields and along the edge of areas of woodland. It may be because I'm too far inland to benefit from the sea breeze but it feels like the hottest day of the whole walk so far. The walking is generally easy going but I'm covered in a clammy sweat as the factor 30 limply melts away.

The path eventually winds its way down to the sea at Rodden Hive and then on to Langton Hive Point, where the views open up ahead of me. I'm now walking the distinctive stretch of path that I had in view towards the end of yesterday, with a strip of water separating me from the endless Chesil Bank to my right. The path clings onto the edge of the flat landscape up against the shoreline. I'm passing through a field of bright yellow oil seed rape when I'm viciously attacked a swarm of, roughly, a gazillion insects. Tiny white flies that appear from amidst the crops and head straight for my face. I flap heroically but there are too many of them. 'Go on without me Rolly, save yourself I (would) cry (if I were as nuts as a bags of nuts).' This merciless assault in broad daylight goes on for a full ten minutes until I reach the end of the field. I regain my composure, spit out the last of the little blighters that flew into my mouth and, dignity intact go about my business.

A little while later I pass the Moonfleet Manor Hotel, named after J Meade Falkner's famous novel Moonfleet. They'd have to be pretty stupid smugglers to conduct their business in this neck of the woods I think to myself as I pick a few deceased white flies from my ears. The flat open landscape doesn't seem very conducive to secret rendezvous' and the stashing of contraband whatnots. A mile or so along the path a military rifle range hones into view. I negotiate my way around it to the sound of gunfire. I seem to have passed as many rifle ranges as golf courses on this trip. As I'm contemplating which of these is the bigger nuisance to the walker, a large caravan site appears up ahead. The holy trinity of coastal fly tipping is complete. The terrain through this section is surprisingly muddy, given the dry weather. I slip and slide my way around

Lynch Cove and round another small fenced off military zone before straightening out, adjacent once more to Chesil Bank.

I soon reach Ferry Bridge and the road that leads to Portland Island. I'm booked into a hotel in Weymouth for two nights, so that I can walk the entire route around the island tomorrow. For now, however, I pass by the road and begin the final few miles into Weymouth itself. This is a boring affair along pavements and through increasingly built up areas. Eventually I arrive at the harbourside and locate my hotel. It sits on the cusp of two very different looking areas. On one side an attractive harbour with rows of sail boats, pretty cottages and ship yards. On the other a high street full of chain pubs and fast food restaurants, waiting for nightfall. Later that evening I venture into the town to locate a laundrette. The trusty old garments need one final detox before the finish line. Whilst they spin themselves into something resembling decency, I grab a bite to eat and sit along the promenade watching the waves lapping against the shore. I stare at the views of the coastline stretching off into the distance and wonder how long now before I see a view of cliffs ahead, that I won't be walking on.

The following day's circular walk around Portland Island begins with the strange feeling of heading off without my backpack. The route starts off with a climb up through a residential area, past the vast and infamous prison. From there I arrive at what, I assume is intended to be some sort of zoo. It is hands down the most depressing zoo I've ever been to. Small groups of kangaroos', goats and a few other assorted animals sit huddled together in featureless enclosed square patches of grass. Everything about their body language screams boredom. A shabby looking goat ambles up to the fence and half-heartedly investigates me before ambling back again, unimpressed.

The trail then winds down to the coastline and I'm pleasantly surprised to discover some decent walking. The

146

route gets quite rocky in places and I get a touch emotional, staring up at a kestrel hovering above. The same question as the previous evening creeps, unwelcome, into my mind; how many more times will I see this now? I watch the beautiful bird until it glides off across the clear blue sky. It's another scorching hot summer day and the sea sparkles enticingly as I continue along the undulating track. I walk through a landslip area and a couple of disused quarries on the long trek towards Portland Bill. I climb back up to the main road at one point and take in some fantastic views, before veering off back down towards sea level again.

When I arrive at Portland Bill the iconic red and white striped lighthouse, with its attached visitor centre, is bustling with tourists enjoying the sunshine. I walk past the crowded cafés and find a spot on the grass to sit and eat lunch. I ungraciously munch down the melted Mars Bar as I stare up at the famous old landmark. I stay here a while enjoying the views back out across Chesil Bank, before deciding to crack on. There are impressive views all along the route back towards Ferry Bridge. The walking itself however is a little less inspiring on this side of the island. Some pleasant hillside strolling eventually succumbs to the built up residential areas of, first Weston, and then Chiswell. I'm not complaining though, it's been a much more enjoyable walk than I was expecting if I'm honest. As I make my way through Chiswell I pass several cars displaying the same bumper sticker; 'Keep Portland Weird', which warms me to the place even more.

I arrive back at Ferry Bridge a few hours earlier than I expected to; the lack of backpack giving me at least an extra half mile an hour. I decide therefore to take the stroll back into Weymouth rather than getting the bus. Perhaps the repetition of these few miles cancel out the missed half a mile in Plymouth? I get back to Weymouth at mid-afternoon with the sun still shining brightly. I'm struck by how much more attractive the town looks in the daylight. I manage to locate a decent looking pub and wile away the rest of the afternoon in the beer garden, with views out to sea.

Durdle Door, Indian Chip Butties
and the Selfish Armed Forces

Weymouth again looks a lot more attractive in the morning sunshine than it does in the neon glow of the night. I begin the day's 14-mile trek to Lulworth with a stroll along the promenade under a cloudy sky. I pass through Bowleaze Cove with its large and striking, if slightly worse for wear, art deco hotel. The wind is picking up now and from here on things start to become more strenuous. The path begins to rise and fall as it hugs the cliff edge. The Jurassic Coast continues to reveal its grandiose beauty at the summit of each climb. The views begin to open up ahead as Weymouth fades away behind me.

Early on I meet a large group of ramblers travelling in the opposite direction, on their way to Portland. We swap a few stories regards what immediately awaits us in either direction and comment on the somewhat alarming rate at which the cliff edge is visibly eroding along this stretch. Huge chunks of muddy earth being ripped away from the landscape and sliding into the watery abyss below. Great tears in the ground beneath our feet, that provide the most visually dramatic example of coastal erosion I've yet witnessed. I then lap up their praise like a needy child upon telling them how far I've come, and continue on my way filled with a gratifyingly inflated sense of self-importance. A feeling which sustains me over the next few miles, as the path levels out for a spell of easy clifftop walking until I eventually roll into Osmington Mills, where I stop for lunch.

The afternoon yields more of the Jurassic Coasts visual splendour and some of the most enjoyable and challenging walking of the last few days. The chalky white cliffs climbing and dropping with increased intensity, as the strong winds continue to enrage the waves beneath me. By the time I've climbed the awesome White Nothe I'm exhausted, but loving every minute of it. The views back to Portland behind me, across the raging sea, are stunning. The moody skies are full of lightning quick gulls, criss-crossing amongst the clouds above me. The path winds down to the impressive Bat's Head; a jagged triangular rock jutting out from amidst the crashing waves.

Late in the day I approach arguably the south coast's most famous and popular landmark. The natural limestone arch that is Durdle Door attracts a plethora of tourists from far and wide, and as it comes into view, the path becomes increasingly more inhabited. In spite of walking through so many bustling tourist towns and villages in the last few weeks, it's still something of a shock to see such a wide demographic of punters adorning the path. Families with pushchairs, folks sporting trainers, smart shoes and even the occasional high heel, noticeably outnumber my fellow sturdy boot and thick socked wanderers. Delighted dogs of every variety bound and splash around enthusiastically.

I climb down the steep wooden steps onto the beach and sit amongst the crowds, taking in the beauty of nature's architecture. I spend 20 minutes or so watching the world go by; a small group of fishermen sit motionless on the shoreline, couples pose with selfie sticks beneath the archway and optimistic gulls tentatively tip toe between picnicking families. I eventually heave on the pack and lumber onwards. The crowds continue to arrive as I traverse the well-defined pathway away from the beach, and towards the village of Lulworth. I stop only briefly to observe the crowded Lulworth Cove before taking root in the nearest pub, for a well-deserved pint of the local.

My bed for the night is courtesy of a picturesque 16th century inn that bills itself as 'extremely dog friendly' on the website. This is not an overstatement. The canine is lord and master within this friendly and welcoming establishment and outnumbers its human clientele, at a rate that defies all logic. They freely wander the narrow-crooked hallways, adorned with doggy artworks. They lounge contentedly under every table and fill every square foot of fur coated floor space. Later in the evening I sit in the bar area surveying the dinner menu, a seemingly ownerless pooch sprawled out at my feet. I order the enticingly named Indian Chip Butty… how could I not? When it arrives, it's not a disappointment; a mountain of chips covered in curry, atop a chunky slice of toasted bread. I feel certain there is a cheese element also, but I'm not able to visually confirm this amongst the culinary carnage. About half way through I begin to wonder if there is some sort of rosette awarded for successful completion of this dining *event*. I soldier through bravely and amble, bloated and fulfilled, over to the bar for a much needed digestif.

I get chatting to the friendly landlady for a while and, after impressing her wildly with stories of my trip so far, she drops something of a bombshell. 'So, what are you going to do about getting through the rifle range tomorrow? It'll be closed until Saturday.' After a further panicked exchange and some frantic internet searching, I establish that tomorrows section of Coast Path, titled by Rolly as 'Lulworth Rifle Range' (on reflection there may have been a clue in there somewhere) is closed on weekdays for military shooting practice. It's with some degree of quiet despair that I retire to my room a short while later. I eventually fall asleep with the prospect whirling through my mind of missing out on a day of the trail, so close to the end.

A prospect that becomes a reality as I awake to the smell of wet dog and the sounds of joyful wagging tails, thumping excitedly along the corridor walls outside my room, some seven hours later. I plot an alternative route for the day whilst wolfing down (no pun intended) the trusted Weetabix. I take some solace in the fact that the route I map out is considerably longer than both the coastal route I would've walked today, and Rolly's suggested alternative. So, I will at least get a decent days hiking in. I'll walk along quiet country roads to the village of Wareham where I'll pick up an interesting sounding trail called the Purbeck Way. This will then lead me to Corfe, where I'll spend the night before heading back down to the coast the following morning, to rejoin the path proper.

I develop an increasingly embittered opinion of the Armed Forces and their insistence on blocking my path for the paltry purpose of national defence, as I dice with death for the entire morning along the distinctly-unquiet-roads between Lulworth and Wareham. The chipper and friendly locals are keen to let me know their opinions, regards my choice of walking route, via a multitude of colourful hand gestures from behind car windscreens as they swerve to avoid me. Eventually, mercifully, I arrive in Wareham. I locate the river where the trail begins and set off on, what I trust will be a greatly improved afternoon. The Sun beats down as I stroll along the flat river side path and eventually out into farmland and sparse heathland. The going is easy and the views somewhat lacking. Perfectly pleasant, but a touch uninspiring.

I spend much of the time considering this lack of inspiration. Has the Coast Path ruined other walking for me? Today's walk is a decent one, taking in an abundance of wildlife and varied terrain. Yet I'm left cold, wishing I was beside the sea. What this walk doesn't do you see, dear reader, is smack you round the face. It doesn't kick you to the floor and then scream into your earhole to pick yourself back up. It doesn't pin you to a cliff edge or make the hairs on the back of your neck stand on end. It doesn't switch in a second from peaceful serenity to dramatic unforgiving anger. It isn't *alive*.

Things do improve during the afternoon as I catch multiple sightings of deer and pass through a swamp like woodland. Then late on in the day the impressive Corfe Castle comes into view. This ends a flat day on a high and my spirits are enlivened, as I stand and appraise the ancient structure. It's a sight, of course, that the Coast Path would not have shown me. I continue into the village of Corfe itself. I find a pub, order the obligatory local ale and plonk myself in the beer garden, with a decent view of the castle. I call Tasha and my folks and in between my rants regarding the sheer selfishness of the armed forces we discuss, for the first time, the arrangements for my pending return to stinky old reality. I'm vaguely conscious that I'm not really accepting the looming finish line as being a reality just yet. I spend the rest of the evening getting (slightly more than) tipsy in the beer garden, watching a variety of colourful bird's flutter and chirp in the evening sunshine. As the sun sets I slump off to find what will be the last campsite of the trip. I've decided to give the canvas one last outing, against my better judgement. I'd like to be able to say, with a something close to a straight face, that I did a mixture of camping, B&B's, pubs and hotels along the trip.

I walk, groggy eyed, but at pace through Corfe as the sun rises the following morning. Leaving the campsite dwellings in my wake ludicrously early, desperate to get back to the coast and put the previous day's flat inland diversion behind me. It wasn't the worst night's sleep I've had under the canvas and despite, or possibly because of, a Mars Bar breakfast (the breakfast of champions) there's a spring in the step as I march onwards. I follow the Purbeck Way for the first few miles before finally rejoining the path at St Aldhelms Head. I'm greeted by breath-taking views in both directions, including painfully tantalising glimpses of the walk I'd been denied a day prior. As I set off in the direction of Worth Matravers the sky is a clear and cloudless blue, and the Sun beats down on my rejuvenated bones.

A few minutes later I spy a buzzard circling above over the grassy cliff edge that separates me from the calm, shimmering blue ocean. After consulting Rolly I'm advised that in actual fact, many of the buzzard sightings I've had could well have been marsh harriers. The one bird I thought I did actually recognise. The familiar chorus of a thousand invisible song birds caresses the sky and raises my spirits even further. I'm filled with the comforting sensation of being home, a feeling of relief at being back on the trail after only 24 hours away. This brings about a brief panic at the pending journey's end, but I quickly push these thoughts aside before they can take root.

Somewhere before, or around Durlston Head, I come across an archetypal SWCP climb. A steep, stepped descent from clifftop down to sea level and the corresponding climb back up immediately afterwards. A broad smile fills my face. It's a sight that only a few months ago would have filled me with dread and brought about the obligatory backpack lamenting whinge-fest. Here and now however, it sends a wave of excitement and adrenalin through me. Bring it on. Before I begin the descent, I pass a young couple sat on a bench on the clifftop. In other circumstances, their sweaty red faces and ungainly panting would have led me to believe I'd crassly interrupted a moment of secret passion. They both smile at me and then grimace at the sight of my backpack. 'It's as tough as it looks; good luck with that pack!' I smile back, possibly a touch smugly, but resist the temptation to set them straight and explain that this is child's play to a seasoned pro like myself... because that would make me sound like a bit of a twonk. I clamber down the uneven steps at pace and climb up the other side without pausing for breath. Upon reaching the top I continue, exhilarated and drenched in sweat. I resist the temptation to turn and wave triumphantly at the couple on the bench... because that would make me look like a bit of a twonk.

A little while later I sling off my backpack and sit looking out to sea, and up at the circling gulls as they glide and weave gracefully, surveying their domain. As I watch them I'm surprised to feel a tear rolling down my cheek. Not a noisy overblown sob you understand dear reader, if anything probably quite heroic and manly tears. It suddenly feels as though this has been coming for days. This incredible adventure is all but at an end and I suppose the reality of that is at last sinking in. I desperately miss Tasha, my family and my friends and will be over the moon to be with them again, but this has been an even more enriching and beautiful experience than I ever could have hoped for. I'll miss the nomadic freedom, the feeling of being on an endless journey. As previously said; life concentrated into its purest and most simple form. Walk, eat, walk, sleep, repeat.

I drink in the horizon as though it's my last, the beautiful and silent sea glistens in the sunlight and I am a tiny dot on the cliff edge. The dramatic ever changing, yet eternal and constant, coastline stretches off into infinity in either direction. Every beautiful square foot of this landscape that I've encountered in the last eight weeks will continue to play out its daily drama centuries after I'm gone, as was the case for centuries past. My epic journey is no more than a passing moment. This living, breathing coastline will not miss me as I will miss it. I regain my composure and continue on my way, ending the days walk with a gentle stroll down the promenade into Swanage and the last B&B of the trip.

Swanage is also the last of the familiar south coast seaside towns on this trip. As I wander down the promenade later that night, past the amusement arcades and fish 'n' chip shops in the evening sunshine, I come across a melee of people gathered around a woman with a microphone and a few cameramen. The

BBC is filming for the local news programme. I phone my mum, who lives on the south coast, and tell her to switch on the TV. I then proceed to move on tip toes through the crowd, waving my arms in the air like a demented idiot. It soon becomes apparent that the filming isn't live and my mum has no idea what I'm blithering on about.

The Last Day

I wake ready for the last day in a numb daze of denial. A short seven-mile walk including the final stretch across the sandy beach of Studland Bay, to South Haven Point. I move slower than I've done in two months to prolong the final hours and wallow in the dying embers of my adventure. Reality awaits me and I feel in no hurry to greet it. As I leave Swanage heading for the impressive Old Harry's Rock, with its characteristic white cliffs, I'm deep in thought. I try to contemplate why this trip has meant so much to me, and why every bone in my body is now crying out at me to turn around and walk the whole path back to Minehead.

A few months prior to the start of the walk I was at a corporate conference event through work. I work in the finance industry and, on that day, was sat in a room with three hundred or so colleagues all talking enthusiastically about the banking industry. Its potential future, its current challenges etc. A variety of speakers took to the stage throughout the day, pushing with genuine enthusiasm the current mantras of the organisation and discussing how we can all achieve great things for ourselves, our business and our customers. There was a moment during the afternoon, whilst pretending to listen and praying that nobody would ask me to venture an opinion on anything being said; that I suddenly asked myself a question. What decisions have I made in my life that have lead me to be in this room with these people? Seriously, how has this happened?

The company I work for has treated me very well and many of the people I work with are amongst my dearest friends. I have no cause for complaint whatsoever and would not say a bad word against my employer. Yet the truth remains that of every known subject on this Earth, you could search for a lifetime and not discover one that interests me less than economics and banking. Seriously, I'm more interested in crocheting. So how am I here? Have I really made a lifetime of bad choices? Every time I've met a fork in the road have I really picked the wrong path? No. The truth is much, much worse.

Every decision I've made in my life has been founded on apathy and fear. I have, on every single occasion, picked the path of least resistance. The easy route. So there I was; an overweight, unhealthy, stressed out insomniac pushing forty. Sat in a conference hall pretending to be someone I'm not and with nobody to blame but myself. By this point I had already discovered a passion for walking and I'm certain it was because of this that I was now asking myself these questions. There was actually something in my life now that inspired me and pushed me, something I wanted, and it had given me perspective.

These are the reasons that this trip has meant so much to me. Because I made it happen, I achieved it. It wasn't the easy route, either literally or figuratively. It's been a physical and mental challenge but it's also something that most of my peers simply don't understand. As I think about all of this, four major conflicting emotions rage within me. Immense pride at having walked 630 miles on my own, a sense of foreboding at returning to the real world and having to summon the strength to then make the changes I need to in my everyday life, overwhelming joy at being with my loved ones again and a total and profound sadness that this incredible experience is ending.

I sub consciously begin muttering a mantra under my breath: *This is who I am, this is what I am, this is why I am, my reason and where I belong. I will not go quietly.* Passers-by, of whom there are many along this popular and accessible final section, become increasingly alarmed at the leather skinned muddy ne'er-do-well with the oversized backpack audibly chanting and staring out to sea. They move their children and dogs away from me to safety. By the time I reach the Pinnacles and Harry I'm still whispering it: *This is who I am, this is what I am, this is why I am, my reason and where I belong. I will not go quietly.* I stand for 40 minutes on the iconic chalky cliff edge gazing out at the horizon. Attempting to summon up a mental montage of my trip – I want an emotional slow motion run through of my experiences in sepia tone with Carter USM's version of The Impossible Dream playing in the background. But I cannot do it. Something in my brain has protectively shut itself down and I can only see the sea, *my sea*, gently swaying off into infinity. Even the (manly) tears of the previous day will not appear; I'm in shut down, as if my brain has crossed the finish line before my feet.

I begrudgingly trudge on towards the beach. As I reach it I come across a cafe and sit, consuming a strawberry milkshake. The place is packed to the rafters with screaming children and stressed parents, out for a day at the beach on a sunny Saturday. Real life is bleeding into my trip and I don't feel ready for it yet. A mile further down the beach I take off my backpack and sit on the sand, in the quietest spot I can find. As I unsheathe the final Mars Bar of the trip, a naked elderly overweight gentleman appears, striding purposefully from the sand dunes behind me, and stops a few feet in front of me facing out to sea. He stands legs apart and hands on hips, the image of his fluorescent white saggy buttocks burning itself

157

onto my retina. Suddenly I'm not hungry and I place the Mars Bar back into my bag where it will remain, ceremoniously uneaten. I've inadvertently wandered into the naturist section of the beach. Over the next half hour or so I come to understand that the naturist community (of this beach at least) is very nearly exclusively made up of aged overweight men. I'm full of admiration for their bravado – 'That's right sonny boy... I'm naked, what of it!' I wonder what they do during the week, are they accountants, tree surgeons and cashiers? Do they represent a broad cross section of society or are there professions that are top heavy with naturists? These questions and many more remain unanswered.

Eventually I stroll on, walking out to where the waves gently lap at the shoreline and wash over my tired and cracked boots. In this final mile, I meet the last person of the trip. A girl in jean-shorts and a straw hat, walking in the opposite direction, sporting a correctly sized backpack and wearing an excited smile on her face.

'Hello' she beams.

'Have you been walking the Coast Path?'

We exchange pleasantries and it transpires she is just starting out and is also going to attempt the full 630 miles.

'I'm envious of you; you've got an amazing two months ahead of you.' I say.

'Two months?! Oh, no I'll be doing it in five weeks at the most.'

'Sure, five weeks, that's what I meant to say.'

As I reach the end of the beach and the last ferry crossing of the journey, the finishing line sculpture comes into view. A blue steel affair stood next to a wooden waymarker, advising that Minehead is 630 miles in the other direction. I again briefly consider walking all the way back, before taking a clumsy selfie that cuts off the top my head. Luckily, at that moment a (fully clothed) man walks past and volunteers to take my picture for me. As I stand reviewing the photograph in the hot May sunshine, I reflect on how different the face staring back at me is to the one in the corresponding picture taken in Minehead, eight weeks prior.

I'm at least a stone-and-a-half lighter and feel fitter than I have done in two decades. I've also slept at least seven hours a night for the majority of the last eight weeks and feel sharper and stronger as a result. I do, however, have a grey streak in my hair that wasn't there previously and as we've discussed dear reader, my skin looks like it's made of old leather. The baby faced, pasty, wheezing couch potato has been replaced by a thin, weathered old man. Swings and roundabouts, I suppose.

As I cross the water for the final time my spirits are brightened at the prospect of the welcoming committee that awaits me on the other side. Tasha, my mum and my stepdad Dennis have driven to meet me, and I'm suddenly overcome with excitement at the thought of seeing them. I have 700 photographs to show them and a thousand stories to tell, the lucky devils! Upon meeting my reception party congratulations and a few final photographs ensue. My mum, delighted to find me alive and well and not butchered at the hands of a crazed old Cornish fisherman, comments instead on my resemblance to aforementioned crazed old Cornish fisherman.

We drive back to mum and Dennis' house where we meet my brother Mark and his partner Tom for dinner. I spend the next few hours regaling them all with stories from the trip; my favourite spots, the most difficult stretches and the folk I met along the way. That spectacular, inspiring, dramatic and life affirming coastline, stretching out into infinity. I thank my mum for resisting the temptation to spend her and Dennis' life savings on a boat so that she could follow me around for the last two months; ensuring I don't fall off a cliff or run out of clean pants. As we all feast I watch Tasha laughing with my brother and look at my wonderful mum making a fuss of everyone. I beam with complete joy as I bask in the glow and warmth of their company.

I have done it: 8 weeks, 630 miles, 26,719 steps, 921 stiles, 302 bridges, 91,000 feet of climbing and descending. 1 family of Seals, 0 basking sharks, 1 Slush puppy, 4 Rolly's and 1 overweight, oversized backpack. Not bad for a pasty podge face pushing forty.

Epilogue

Every now and then, when I'm driving, working, eating a potato or lying awake thinking about death... Or maybe even hiking somewhere inland across a moor or through woodlands; the sea calls to me. No matter what time it is or how far away from it I am, I go to it. Travelling 40, 50, 100 miles out of my way to be with it. To walk the path at Sidmouth in the driving rain, or Combe Martin in a dense winter fog. I suspect that the most likely reason for this is that I unintentionally left a layer of my consciousness on the Coast Path, when I returned to normal life. Abandoned to forever walk the trail back and forth between Minehead and Poole Harbour. From time to time, whatever signal it's emitting hits the right frequency at the right moment to find me.

Then, when I reach the sea, the splintered layer of consciousness temporarily re-attaches itself to me and as the smell, sound and feel of the sea penetrate my senses; I am whole again. An almost unbearable wave of happiness washes through me. Oddly, every time this happens I realise that in the time that has elapsed since I was last with the sea, I have forgotten that I'm not whole and that this level of happiness is possible. Life has filled my head with electricity bills, pasta bakes, Netflix, stress, spreadsheets, referendums and decay. The sea tells me again that all this is a fiction; a meaningless and elaborate construction. It shows me that life is simple, clear and endlessly beautiful. I thank the sea and walk beside it for a time. Just as my spirit begins to dance and my heart is about to burst with purist joy, the splintered layer of consciousness leaves me again so that I can begin the journey back, to the other reality. By the time I arrive my thoughts have turned to food shopping, team meetings, mini-breaks and overdrafts. I cannot hear the sea now, but I belong to it, and it will find me.

A few of the words I've used far too much due to insufficient vocabulary:
Undulating
Majestic
Shimmering
Turquoise
Ascent/Descent
Dramatic
Jagged

Stephen Reynolds Presents: *Let's Get Ready to Ramble.*

An LP of Walking-Themed Classics

Full Track Listing:
1) Get Ready to Ramble
2) Going Coastal (Down in Porthcurno)
3) Let's Talk About Exe Baby
4) Keep Strollin', Strollin', Strollin'
5) (Do You Know the Way to) Booby's Bay
6) Looe Changes Everything
7) (I was) Born on the SWCP
8) Striders on the Storm
9) Walking on the Dock of the Bay
10) Walking 9 to 5 (not to make a living)

Rejected Book Title Ideas:
1) National Trail – ing Diaries *(Say it out loud... Pretty funny yeah? Oh, please yourselves)*
2) Walking it off
3) Is it for Charity?
4) A Moving Dot *(I like this one, but it's a bit... well, plonkerish)*
5) Something to Do

Lightning Source UK Ltd.
Milton Keynes UK
UKHW010710080319
338729UK00008B/137/P